CW00797846

Borderless
Envisioning and Experiencing One Church Community of Believers Without Walls, Borders and Denominations

Ambassador Monday O. Ogbe

"From the first Day of Pentecost, the Holy Spirit has proven that He will only come to the degree that we have unity" – Rick Joyner

Dedication

I dedicate this book to the Lord Jesus Christ that prayed, "..*I have given them the glory that you give me, that they may be one as we are one..*"- *John 17:22* and showed me the vision of His divided body on the 22nd of April 2006 with a burden for unity in the body of Christ.

About the book

If you take a look around our world today, walls are being erected everywhere between continents, countries, communities and families. Even the Church of our Lord and Savior Jesus Christ is not spared out of segregation and denominational divides right in our very midst.

This book, *Borderless – Envisioning and experiencing one church community of believers without walls, borders and denominations* is about unity in the body of Christ. It is calling the church to a place of unity of Spirit in response to Jesus prayer *that they may be one...John 17:22*. A call to our various gathering to strive for unity. That we will all envision and experience a borderless church without walls, borders and denomination. A church that despite diversity will be united in spirit and engage as one as written in Ephesians 4:5-6 King James Version (KJV)
5 One Lord, one faith, one baptism,6 One God and Father of all, who is above all, and through all, and in you all.

No more denominational walls and borders. Just one denomination - Jesus Christ, Our Lord and savior taking His place as the only supreme head of His church. It is an appeal and prayer to unity, to oneness, to love and to one body in one Christ Jesus. If after reading the book and you become burdened to the point of engagement with our other brothers and sisters in love in other gathering beyond your own familiar domain, creed, doctrine and denomination, then the book will have done its job and my job will have been dispensed.

"Being prideful means having or showing an arrogant superiority to and disdain of that one view as unworthy. Pride can only be found where there is no love. Where there is no love, there is no God because God is love. Our love for God is the root while our love for the brethren is the fruit. Jesus says, a Christian will be known by the fruit of love they manifest. The world will know us by the love we have for one another." – Monday Ogwuojo Ogbe

"A House divided against itself cannot stand - True! Whether it is the family, Church or Nation! May the good Lord show us mercy and cause us to guard against the little foxes that subtly disrupts what is good. We pray for unity of purpose in Jesus name!" – Sola Ogunnaike.

"Thank you, Monday, for this exposition. The church of Jesus Christ need to realize that the greatest message of love we send to the unbelieving world is our working in unity" – Grace Akuh.

"We all need one another to be the complete reflection of Him." – Rick Joyner

"Thank you for taking on the presentation of the church history and how we got divided. I like the rich passages and perceptive insights. They are very useful." – Dr. Daniel Obaka

"Has it ever occurred to you that one hundred pianos all tuned to the same fork are automatically tuned to each other? They are of one accord by being tuned, not to each other, but to another standard to which each one must individually bow. So one hundred worshippers together, each one looking away to Christ, are in heart nearer to each other than they could possibly be were they to become 'unity' conscious and turn their eyes away from God to strive for closer fellowship."- A.W. Tozer, (*The Pursuit of God*)

"It is high time we do something about disunity in the body of Christ. Thank you for sharing information on other Christian groups and how we can connect with them" – Vera Atodo

"A true non-denominational view holds that the body of Christ cannot be and should not be denominated"

About the author

Monday Ogwuojo Ogbe is a marketplace ambassador of Christ with a heart for unity in the body of Christ. His face to face encounter with the Lord Jesus Christ on the 22nd of April 2006 changed the trajectory of His life forever.

As an ICT expert, he uses His skill to reach online seekers and equip the body of Christ to the work of ministry via his website otakada.org where over 2 million Christian focused content are now hosted and distributed to a worldwide audience of both seekers and Christians.

He has written several books namely Borderless - Envisioning and experiencing one church community of believers without walls, borders and denomination; Escape to a world of understanding – antidote to hatred against Muslims Christians and people everywhere; Win Life's Battle Daily – a daily declaration of scripture geared to winning life daily; Engaging the Supernatural God – God is eager to speak are we hungry to speak?; Ignite the raw fire power within you – Where the Holy Spirit is available to do exploits through us and Break free revival prayers of 12 series from January to December – Praying for revival in our life's in the church community around us.

Link to books on amazon –

https://www.amazon.com/s?k=Ambassador+Monday+O.Ogbe&crid=17AKQF9MSV26I&sprefix=ambassador+monday+o.ogbe%2Caps%2C454&ref=nb_sb_noss

He publishes a weekly blog that reaches audience on social media, Satellite broadcast and on his publishing website otakada.org.

Blog link:

https://www.otakada.org/category/blog/

He is married to Comfort and has four children namely Diana Odjo, Joseph - Ojima, David - Ojonogwa and Isaac - Unekwu

About the Publisher – Otakada.org

About Us – Gods Eagle Ministries – We Envision A United Christian World! John 17:21-23!

Evangelism, Discipleship, Counseling, Healing, Deliverance, Restoration and Prayer without Walls, Borders and Denominations!

Welcome to about us at Gods Eagle Ministries – We Envision A United Christian World! John 17:21-23! – We are Seeding The Nations with God's WORD, and God Himself is Transforming Lives Through the Timeless Truth in His Word – One Content at a time! – We are ONE in Christ Jesus, let's stay ONE!

At God's Eagle Ministries – We Envision A United Christian World! John 17:21-23! We are seeding the Nations with Over 2 Million Christian Centric Content, and God is Transforming Lives Through the Timeless Truth in His Word – One Content at a Time! – We are ONE in Christ Jesus, let's stay ONE!

Evangelism, Discipleship, Counseling, Healing, Deliverance, Restoration and Prayer without Walls, Borders and Denominations!

Together with YOU, we are building MASSIVE SPIRITUAL TEMPLES in OUR HEARTS for the Spirit of God to DWELL in and OPERATE through

with EASE in these TIMES and SEASONS, so STAY with us and BUILD with us as God Heals, Delivers, and Restores our Spirit, Soul and Body In Jesus Name, Amen!

Check this out in 1 Thessalonians 5:23, 2 Timothy 1:7 Hebrews 4:12-13; 1 Corinthians 3: 1- 17; Leviticus 26:12; Jeremiah 32:38; Ezekiel 37:27; 2 Corinthians 6:16; 1 John 4:4

Read – 1 Thessalonians 5:23 Amplified Bible (AMP) [23] Now may the God of peace Himself sanctify you through and through [that is, separate you from profane and vulgar things, make you pure and whole and undamaged—consecrated to Him—set apart for His purpose]; and may your spirit and soul and body be kept complete and [be found] blameless at the coming of our Lord Jesus Christ.

Who is God's Eagle ministries and What do we do –
Who We are at God's Eagle Ministries, is tied to our vision, mission and values as highlighted hereunder:

Our Vision:
Short Vision: We envision a UNITED Christian World through Christ Centered – Obedience based Disciple Making

Expanded – We envision a UNITED Christian World where Unity of Spirit is maintained through peace and the Unity of FAITH is ATTAINED through equipping in obedience based discipleship and in the accurate knowledge and revealed word of our Lord Jesus Christ by the Holy Spirit

Our Mission:
Short Mission: We are One in Christ Jesus – We exist to Foster Unity of Spirit and Faith Amongst the Saints

Enlarged – All our resources in partnership with the five-fold ministry gifts in the body of Christ, will be geared towards Creating, Collating, and Circulating Christian Content (CCCCC) for the discipling and equipping of the saints till we all maintain the unity of SPIRIT through the bond of peace and attain the unity of FAITH and the knowledge of our Lord Jesus Christ in all nations of the earth as the Holy Spirit leads us

Scriptures that form the bedrock of the ministry – Ephesians 4:3,13; Psalm 133:1; John 17:21; Matthew 28:19; John 8:31 and John 16:13

Our Values:
Boldness, Fearlessness, Leadership, Excellence, Integrity, Creativity, Speed and Charity

Our Passion:
We are passionately, passionate to engage with leadership across denominational lines or across non-denominational lines, urging them to engage with one another, we communicate what the Spirit is saying to the churches and leadership as we intercede for the church and leadership. We pray without ceasing, we see, we experience and we encourage the maintaining of the unity of SPIRIT by the bond of peace through the help of His Holy Spirit in and amongst the saints of God in Christ Jesus according to Jesus prayer in John 17:21 – That we will be one! We also create our

contents and we collate, and circulate Christian contents from the five-fold ministry from different churches and distribute them so that the saints are well equipped until we all come to the unity of faith and of the knowledge of our Lord Jesus Christ as we maintain unity of SPIRIT in the bond of peace – Ephesians 4:3,13

OUR GOAL

Our goal at God's Eagle Ministries is to effectively engage 100 million souls in discipleship on or before 2040 as the Lord tarries...stay with us.

Seven (7) Outplay of what we do:

- Engagement with the message of Unity to the Churches: We engage with different denomination urging them to engage with one another
- Annual Prayer and Fasting: Every year, we dedicate 40 days as instructed by the Lord between March 17th to April 26th to intercede for the Church and Leadership with the core theme of unity, revival and discipleship
- We have published over 65 discipleship books authored by us. We have also published for other Christian authors over 100 titles and distributed to 66 countries
- We have created by ourselves, collated from other five-fold ministries gifts in different denominations and circulated from our website over 2 million Christian contents to equip the saints in the nations
- We have created and automated 40 days' discipleship process with Jesus on our website at Otakada.org with hundreds of visitors from all around the world gaining access to the portal.
- We are counseling Christians from around the world who come in contact with us on our website and through other ministry engagement with other church denominations as God brings healing, deliverance and restoration to His people both in their spirit, soul and body.
- Prophetic Action as led by the Holy Spirit: We carry out prophetic actions as the Holy Spirit leads dedicating the land to the Lord where we function.

You can partner with what we do by visiting our partnership page https://www.otakada.org/partnership-giving/ visit https://shop.otakada.org for eBooks and paperback to help you grow in the lord

Distilling Further, Our Mission at God's Eagle Ministries ties in with Ephesians 4:1-16, to seek out the best of the best five (5) fold ministry gifts in the body of Christ, so that we can equip the saints for the work of Ministry (Laborers are few indeed, whilst there are ripe harvest of souls all around us waiting to be harvested) equipping continues till we all come to the unity of faith as loudly proclaimed in the place of prayer by Jesus Himself in John 17 And the knowledge of our Lord Jesus Christ.

Our core passion is to point the saints, who are sons of our Father God to Christ, who is the head of the body according to the order of

John 1:12-13

Amplified Bible, Classic Edition

[12] But to as many as did receive and welcome Him, He gave the authority (power, privilege, right) to become the children of God, that is, to those who believe in (adhere to, trust in, and rely on) His name—

[13] Who owe their birth neither to bloods nor to the will of the flesh [that of physical impulse] nor to the will of man [that of a natural father], but to God. [They are born of God!]

John 3:12-20

Amplified Bible, Classic Edition

[12] If I have told you of things that happen right here on the earth and yet none of you believes Me, how can you believe (trust Me, adhere to Me, rely on Me) if I tell you of heavenly things?

[13] And yet no one has ever gone up to heaven, but there is One Who has come down from heaven—the Son of Man [Himself], [a]Who is (dwells, has His home) in heaven.

[14] And just as Moses lifted up the serpent in the desert [on a pole], so must [so it is necessary that] the Son of Man be lifted up [on the cross],

[15] In order that everyone who believes in Him [who cleaves to Him, trusts Him, and relies on Him] may [b]not perish, but have eternal life and [actually] live forever!

[16] For God so greatly loved and dearly prized the world that He [even] gave up His only begotten ([c]unique) Son, so that whoever believes in (trusts in, clings to, relies on) Him shall not perish (come to destruction, be lost) but have eternal (everlasting) life.

[17] For God did not send the Son into the world in order to judge (to reject, to condemn, to pass sentence on) the world, but that the world might find salvation and be made safe and sound through Him.

[18] He who believes in Him [who clings to, trusts in, relies on Him] is not judged [he who trusts in Him never comes up for judgment; for him there is no rejection, no condemnation—he incurs no damnation]; but he who does not believe (cleave to, rely on, trust in Him) is judged already [he has already been convicted and has already received his sentence] because he has not believed in and trusted in the name of the only begotten Son of God. [He is condemned for refusing to let his trust rest in Christ's name.]

[19] The [basis of the] judgment (indictment, the test by which men are judged, the ground for the sentence) lies in this: the Light has come into the world, and people have loved the darkness rather than and more than the Light, for their works (deeds) were evil.

[20] For every wrongdoer hates (loathes, detests) the Light, and will not come out into the Light but shrinks from it, lest his works (his deeds, his activities, his conduct) be exposed and reproved.
John 14:1-17

Amplified Bible, Classic Edition

14 Do not let your hearts be troubled (distressed, agitated). You believe in and adhere to and trust in and rely on God; believe in and adhere to and trust in and rely also on Me.

[2] In My Father's house there are many dwelling places (homes). If it were not so, I would have told you; for I am going away to prepare a place for you.

[3] And when (if) I go and make ready a place for you, I will come back again and will take you to Myself, that where I am you may be also.

[4] And [to the place] where I am going, you know the way.

[5] Thomas said to Him, Lord, we do not know where You are going, so how can we know the way?

[6] Jesus said to him, I am the Way and the Truth and the Life; no one comes to the Father except by (through) Me.

[7] If you had known Me [had learned to recognize Me], you would also have known My Father. From now on, you know Him and have seen Him.

[8] Philip said to Him, Lord, show us the Father [cause us to see the Father—that is all we ask]; then we shall be satisfied.

[9] Jesus replied, Have I been with all of you for so long a time, and do you not recognize and know Me yet, Philip? Anyone who has seen Me has seen the Father. How can you say then, Show us the Father?

[10] Do you not believe that I am in the Father, and that the Father is in Me? What I am telling you I do not say on My own authority and of My own accord; but the Father Who lives continually in Me does the ([a]His) works (His own miracles, deeds of power).

[11] Believe Me that I am in the Father and the Father in Me; or else believe Me for the sake of the [very] works themselves. [If you cannot trust Me, at least let these works that I do in My Father's name convince you.]

[12] I assure you, most solemnly I tell you, if anyone steadfastly believes in Me, he will himself be able to do the things that I do; and he will do even greater things than these, because I go to the Father.

[13] And I will do [I Myself will grant] whatever you ask in My Name [as [b]presenting all that I Am], so that the Father may be glorified and extolled in (through) the Son.

[14] [Yes] I will grant [I Myself will do for you] whatever you shall ask in My Name [as [c]presenting all that I Am].

[15] If you [really] love Me, you will keep (obey) My commands.

[16] And I will ask the Father, and He will give you another Comforter (Counselor, Helper, Intercessor, Advocate, Strengthener, and Standby), that He may remain with you forever—

[17] The Spirit of Truth, Whom the world cannot receive (welcome, take to its heart), because it does not see Him or

know and recognize Him. But you know and recognize Him, for He lives with you [constantly] and will be in you.

and Ephesians 1:5

He predestined us to adoption as sons through Jesus Christ to Himself, according to the kind intention of His will

But not as jobless sons but those who are well equipped through core practical oriented Discipleship so that they can launch out as a mighty army to go make disciples of all nations without regards to denomination for we are one in Christ Jesus, amen.

To promote Christ in us – sons of a mighty God, the hope of glory! Colossians 1:26-27 "The Mystery of the kingdom is simply this: Christ in you! Yes, Christ in you bringing with him the hope of all glorious things to come. '" It goes on to say that "the hope of glory is the fulfillment of God's promise to restore us and all creation" – Hallelujah!

To break it down further, Our Passion at God's Eagle Ministries – Otakada.org and the body of Christ, in general, is to equip faith-based communities and to reach online seekers through wholesome content, products, and services that enhance holistically the spirit, the soul, and the body of the individual and to foster unity in the body of Christ!

The Unity of the Spirit and the Unity of the Faith what is the difference?

1. "Using diligence to keep the unity of the Spirit in the uniting bond of peace" (Ephesians 4:3).

2. "Until we all arrive at the unity of the faith and of the knowledge of the Son of God" (Ephesians 4:13).

THE UNITY OF THE SPIRIT—It is important to notice that we are not told to make this unity, but to use diligence to keep it. The unity already is; but in a practical way—not in strife, but in the uniting bond peace, we are to walk accordingly, in love to "all the saints." There are various influences at work to mar this, but "the uniting bond of peace "is the practical answer to them all. The authority of the Lord, and the gracious direction and ministry of our exalted Head, will be abundantly realized by those who thus endeavour, apart from sects and schools, to keep the unity of the Spirit.

THE UNITY OF THE FAITH, in verse 13, is another matter. The activity of the gifts has the edifying of the body of Christ in view to this end: "Until we all arrive at the unity of the faith, and of the knowledge of the Son of God." We must not confound the two. This is objective, whereas the unity of the Spirit is more subjective, involving the vital oneness of the members of the body of Christ. The unity of the Faith is something which the saints are to come to, or "arrive at," in connection with the knowledge of the Son of God.

He has made a perfect revelation, and in this, known in Him alone—in Him whose words, and ways, and works, have so fully and blessedly declared the Father, His own become one in the Father and the Son. Here indeed we need to advance, to grow in the excellent knowledge of our Lord Jesus Christ, the blessed Son of God, into the fellowship of whom God has graciously called us.

THE UNITY OF THE SPIRIT—Much has been said as to this which leaves the impression on the mind that it is something to be made or something to be attained to, instead of something to be kept, as we have said, in a practical way—in "the uniting bond of peace." We must cease from denominating beloved saints of God by party and divisive names which are a shame to us. The practice is not only a careless one, but a sinful one; for we are all members of Christ's body, and we must acknowledge no other membership, even if others do. Let us then, for the sake of the One who loves all His own perfectly, speak and think of one another becomingly, and be ashamed of these party names which have no right to exist, for Christ cannot be divided. This will greatly help towards practical unity in the bond of peace. The endeavouring we are exhorted to is on this line. We are to be "using diligence," but special effort having some favoured party in view is not here contemplated. Our efforts must be governed by the truth in regard to the whole position, or they will militate against the unity of the Spirit.

It has been said, "The unity of the Spirit is that which is already formed and embraces all the members of Christ," and again, It is "the common place which pertains to all the children of God" (W.K.).

Another wrote, "It is not only abstractedly, but actually one, forming one body, putting each member in its place in the body"; also, on my side, "If love to all the saints is not present in my spirit, I break (the unity) … while keeping it up in form"; for it is "not similarity of sentiment, but the oneness of the members of the body of Christ established by the Holy Ghost" (J.N.D.). Where healthful diligence is in activity as to this established unity, and also advance is being made in regard to the unity of the faith, and of the knowledge of our blessed Lord and Saviour as the Son of God, rich results will necessarily follow for God's glory.

"UNITY"—Twice only is the word found in our New Testament; in Ephesians 4:3, and 13; and but once in the Old Testament. There it is significantly used in the last Song of Degrees but one; just before the Lord is blessed in the sanctuary, and His blessing flows out of Zion (Ps. 134). Mark the Spirit's words: "Behold, how good and how pleasant it is for brethren to dwell together in unity (Ps. 133). It is like the precious ointment which is not only upon the Head, but which reaches to all connected with Him, whilst the fragrant perfume of it pervades all around. It is also like the dew of Hermon's height: descending, distilling, and refreshing Zion. No wonder we read, "There the Lord commands the blessing—even eternal life!" It is not surprising that this is the only place eternal life is mentioned in the O.T. except Daniel 12:2

"Behold how good and how pleasant it is for BRETHREN TO DWELL TOGETHER IN UNITY."

Shall we not seek this with diligence? It is to be our portion for ever in the Father's house, with Him who is the Firstborn among many brethren.

Shalom!

Ambassador Oreojo Monday Ogwuojo Ogbe

About Us – Gods Eagle Ministries – Otakada Inc – A United Christian World

Acknowledgement

I acknowledge God the Father, Son and the Holy Spirit that gave me this burden for unity in the body of Christ and propel me to write to the body of Christ to come together as one body. Thank You Father, Son and the Holy Spirit.

Preface

Borderless – Envisioning and Experiencing One Church Community of believers Without Walls, Borders and Denominations is a burden the lord put upon me after a vision I received on Saturday, the 22nd of April 2006, 5 am in the morning during 40 days fast He had instructed me to start, praying for the church and leadership. It was three days to the end of the 40 days fast the vision of the divided body was shown me. I will give account of this in the introductory chapter. Since then, I have written, visited churches and employing them to engage. This book is a collection of writings to our audience on otakada.org blog and social media handle all compressed into this one book. The call to unity is urgent, it is needed not just for ourselves but for those souls that are seeing the division amongst us and would not give their lives to Christ. You will be burdened after reading this book to do something in the mighty name of Jesus Christ, Amen.

Table of Contents

Chapter 1 – Introduction – The Vision of the divided body of Christ

Church activity without real encounter

"**The Father, the Son and the Holy Spirit are one. The Father is not The Son, The Son is not the Holy Spirit, yet they operate and function as one.** The Body is not the Spirit, or is the Spirit the mind but in this part of eternity, all three must work together so we can be a complete human being. The man is not the woman, neither is the woman the man but God said, they are one. **God is interested in who we are and also interested in what we do with who we are.**" – Monday Ogwuojo Ogbe

"**Our first calling is to fellowship, not works.**" – Rick Joyner

I was born into a Christian family, have been a Christian, busy going to church, attending activities and serving as best I could until this encounter that turned my life around. On the 16th of March 2006, I was pacing up and down the hospital hallway in London as my wife had already been in labor for three days. The doctors finally concluded that if she did not have the baby naturally by morning, she would have to undergo a caesarean section. Unknown to us, my mother in law had already seen in a vision that she might not make it through this delivery. Thank God for godly mothers-in-law. Of course, my wife and I did not know about this.

My Encounter

It was during this pacing up and down that I received a strong impression upon my mind to initiate a forty (40) day fast beginning the next day, which was the 17th of March 2006. I was alarmed because I had never carried out a forty-days fast before. This is how you distinguish the fleshy thoughts and thoughts impressed upon you from our heart to our mind by the Holy Spirit in us. He will tell you to do something scriptural that you will not naturally succumb to. I began a conversation with the spontaneous thought lighting upon my mind, thought in response to thought, impressions of what I would be praying about for forty days. Next instruction was that I should pick a jotter and a pen and I began to write right there and then in the hospital ward the impressions I was receiving. Rather than pray for my wife, I found out the prayer points coming to my mind were on pastors, the churches and unity in the body. It was then I asked God, if I were to carry out this task, I would want to see Him before these 40 days fasting ends. There was no response I believe now because the condition for Him manifesting was going to depend on my obedience to the first instruction to fast 40 days.

Obedience is key

A point to note here before I continue the story is that God will not take the next move beyond your last point of obedience. If He instructs you to do something, you don't do it, He shuts down until you get back to the last point of disobedience and obey. Read Jonah's account. Jonah ran in the opposite direction to God's assignment. Through the storms, as long as Jonah was in disobedience, God never spoke, until Jonah, after his futile attempt to commit suicide failed, He cried out to God.

Now the encounter continues: Behold, on the 22nd of April 2006, three days to the end of the forty-days fast at exactly 5 am in the morning, God kept His part of the bargain. I was half awake when this Being, in human form, with His hands folded behind His back, bent forward slightly, looking at me on the floor, walked gently, one step at a time, not in a hurry, walked towards me into the lounge through the window area. I could make out His form but could not see His face clearly. You know the type of dressing Jesus dresses in some of the movies that I had watched. Immediately He came near me, the area around my feet where He was standing began to vibrate with so much force as if it never existed, more like the area just dematerialized so to speak. As He moved towards my chest, neck and head area, same thing happened and He kept going back and forth. Every area He left recombined again as before and the process continues as before. There were no words to describe the raw power of that experience; I lost track of time and I became afraid and began to beg that it would end and He should tell me what he wanted me to do for Him while rolling uncontrollably on the floor. That was my encounter with the manifest power of our heavenly father.

Detailed vision of disunity:

After that trance experience, I began to see different vision of the body of Christ. On one occasion, in the dream, the Lord Jesus Christ walked in, His body was all disjointed but connected with tiny skin ligaments. Each of the parts was a church ministry. I could make out ministries I was familiar with. The connections between the body parts were not firm. I now understand that the church institutions or ministries as we know them today, are dividing His body, the individual members of His church making up His body because of pride, petty ego and all the lust that the flesh presents. Manifesting as Inter-church competition, leadership struggle, diversion of members, running down other ministries, infighting going on between church members, leadership stealing and living flamboyant lifestyle that does not reflect the living standard of members and the list goes on. If you are such, depart from iniquity, because our God is a consuming fire and remember the sin of Balaam who for monetary lust, misrepresented God and handed Gods blessed children unto Satan through evil counsel to the adversary.

I now asked the Lord where I was to fit in this lightly connected disjointed body of His. He told me to look for churches that make disciples of men and that I should not be moved by numbers.

Clarity of purpose

The rest is History. I now realized my confidence in Him was built up after the encounter, I now had a sense of purpose and mission. All the assignment God gave me in subsequent dreams/visions were consistent with this first assignment. There has been no controversy at all. I do sometimes derail, but He lovingly leads me back and sometimes with bruises to show for disobedience. The power and presence of the Holy Spirit has enabled me to accomplish things that I would naturally not be able to in reaching out to specific area of assignment. God fills us with His Holy Spirit to equip us for ministry. Never take on any task for God without the divine enablement and assignment.

Clarity of dialogue

This revelation gave me the confidence and assurance that God is available and more than desirous to engage us in conversation, if we are willing to tune in to His frequency and ask from Him in faith. He speaks through trance (open visions) as in this case, through dreams, through image impressions, spontaneous thought that light upon our minds, through circumstances we face, people we meet, ordained men and women of God, through children, through silence and through the word of God and other variants. It is critical to note that the inner witness and the word of God has to agree with what we have seen, heard or impressed on our mind. Satan and demonic spirit also speak, show and impress upon our minds as well. Satan can masquerade of angel of light so beware.

God speaks, He is still speaking and would continue to speak. We have to be ready to obey His instruction to keep the flow.

Other Jesus messages to the churches on unity to Dale Fife

"Then the voice of the Spirit said, "This is what you have done to My church. You have defiled the purity of My bride. You have torn My beautiful bride into pieces and dismembered her. You have divided the parts of My body and put them on display. You have exalted some of the parts and scorned others. I have watched while you ridicule that which I call holy. My heart is broken. I can bear it no longer."- Dale

"The Lord said, "Behold, they are coming. Even now, they are approaching. Behold, My great company of apostles and prophets. (See 1 Corinthians 12:28; Ephesians 4:11–16.) Some have already begun to work among the body parts to bring healing and restoration to the bride." – Dale Fife

"Jesus spoke with divine admiration, saying, "I have released the apostles of My right hand and the prophets of My left hand to the work for which I have called them. In the days to come, the things that have divided My body will be rooted up and torn down. My Spirit will demolish all that separates and all that seeks to honor one above another, for all are made by My design, and all must be honored. This is the word of the Lord. It shall be done. The structures that are man-made will be shaken and will fall. (See Hebrews 12:25–29.) My true bride, My holy bride, will come forth in all her glory." – Dale Fife

Conclusion

The vision and burden for a borderless church, church without walls or denomination was born out of this encounter. As we go through the writing in the following chapters, may you be burdened to action concerning the work of unity in the body of Christ in Jesus name, Amen.

Chapter 2 - Intimacy in unity of the Spirit

"Some claim to be non-denominational, but are really multi-denominational."

We are exploring how crucially important it is for us, called as intercessors to keep the unity of the Spirit. In fact, it is absolutely impossible to get into and remain in intimacy with our Heavenly Father if there is no bond of peace with fellow believers. When I say believers, I mean believers not defined by same church assembly, ministry or doctrinal agreement but believers all over the world. We cannot be effective in the place of intercession until we remove the vail of denominational affiliation, doctrinal or ministry mindset from our minds. It is hindering soul winning which is the core of our call because no intelligent unbeliever, seeing what is happening amongst believers today will want to join such association.

Key Scripture:

John 17:13-23

13-19 Now I'm returning to you.
I'm saying these things in the world's hearing
So my people can experience
My joy completed in them.
I gave them your word;
The godless world hated them because of it,
Because they didn't join the world's ways,

Just as I didn't join the world's ways.
I'm not asking that you take them out of the world
But that you guard them from the Evil One.
They are no more defined by the world
Than I am defined by the world.
Make them holy—consecrated—with the truth;
Your word is consecrating truth.
In the same way that you gave me a mission in the world,
I give them a mission in the world.
I'm consecrating myself for their sakes
So they'll be **truth-consecrated in their mission.**

20-23 I'm praying not only for them
But also for those who will believe in me
Because of them and their witness about me.
**The goal is for all of them to become one heart and
mind—**
Just as you, Father, are in me and I in you,
So they might be one heart and mind with us.
Then the world might believe that you, in fact, sent me.
The same glory you gave me, I gave them,
So they'll be as unified and together as we are—
I in them and you in me.
Then they'll be mature in this oneness,
And give the godless world evidence
That you've sent me and loved them
In the same way you've loved me.

Ephesians 4:1-6
1 I, therefore, the prisoner of the Lord, beseech you to walk
worthy of the calling with which you were called,
2 with all lowliness and gentleness, with longsuffering,
bearing with one another in love,

3 endeavoring to keep the *unity of the Spirit* in the bond of peace.
4 There is *one body and one Spirit, just as you were called in one hope of your calling; 5 one Lord, one faith, one baptism;*
6 one God and Father of all, who is above all, and through all, and in you all.

The Lord revealed to me twelve (12) years ago that our church organizations are tearing His bride apart with a vivid picture of Himself all divided and appended to these body parts are church organizations as we know them today. This terrible disunity accounts for the powerlessness in miracle crumbs, absence of fruitfulness, greed, pride, epileptic growth and myriads of other unexplainable abnormalities amongst us believers today.

Paul Brand and Philip Yancey in their book, Fearfully and Wonderfully Made, gave a vivid account of this stinking sickness as it relate to the human body..

"USING THE ANALOGY OF THE HUMAN BODY, there are some diseases that can spread infection throughout the body of Christ. The mind can become swollen with pride. The heart can grow cold and indifferent because of sin. The digestive system can get clogged by sterile theory and unapplied theology, so the body can't digest what needs to be turned into energy or eliminate what needs to be released. When that occurs we start to fight among ourselves unable to stay balanced. . . .Sometimes a dreaded thing occurs in the body-a mutiny-resulting in a tumor. . . .

A tumor is called benign if its effect is fairly localized and it stays within membrane boundaries. But the most traumatizing condition in the body occurs when disloyal cells defy inhibition. They multiply without any checks on growth, spreading rapidly throughout the body, choking out normal cells. White cells, armed against foreign invaders, will not attack the body's own mutinous cells. Physicians fear no other malfunction more deeply: it is called cancer. For still mysterious reasons, these cells-and they may be cells from the brain, liver, kidney, bone, blood, skin, or other tissues-grow wild, out of control. Each is a healthy, functioning cell, but disloyal, no longer acting in regard for the rest of the body.

Even the white cells, the dependable palace guard, can destroy the body through rebellion. Sometimes they recklessly reproduce, clogging the blood stream, overloading the lymph system, strangling the body's normal functions-such is leukemia.

Because I am a surgeon and not a prophet, I tremble to make the analogy between cancer in the physical body and mutiny in the spiritual body of Christ. But i must. In his warnings to the church, Jesus Christ showed no concern about the shocks and bruises His body would meet from external forces. "The gates of Hell shall not prevail against my church," He said flatly (Matthew 16:18). He moved easily, unthreatened, among sinners and criminals. But He cried out against the kind of disloyalty that comes from within."

Here are comments from Christ Himself to let us know how terrible the Lord views anything and anyone that divides His bride. Judgement has already started and will

continue until perfection, until the wall that is tearing the bride apart crumbles, until what matters to all of us is our intimate relationship with our Heavenly Father.
Hear Jesus speaking out on disunity in His body:

1)Then the voice of the Spirit said, "This is what you have done to My church. You have defiled the purity of My bride. You have torn My beautiful bride into pieces and dismembered her. You have divided the parts of My body and put them on display. You have exalted some of the parts and scorned others. I have watched while you ridicule that which I call holy. My heart is broken. I can bear it no longer."

2) The Lord said, "Behold, they are coming. Even now, they are approaching. Behold, My great company of apostles and prophets. (See 1 Corinthians 12:28; Ephesians 4:11–16.) Some have already begun to work among the body parts to bring healing and restoration to the bride."

3) Jesus spoke with divine admiration, saying, "I have released the apostles of My right hand and the prophets of My left hand to the work for which I have called them. In the days to come, the things that have divided My body will be rooted up and torn down. My Spirit will demolish all that separates and all that seeks to honor one above another, for all are made by My design, and all must be honored. This is the word of the Lord. It shall be done. The structures that are man-made will be shaken and will fall. (See Hebrews 12:25–29.) My true bride, My holy bride, will come forth in all her glory."

Let him who have ears hear what the Spirit of the living God is saying to the churches.

Prayer of intercession for the bride of Christ from my heart :- I earnestly intercede for the body of Christ today and always, represented as the bride of Christ, created in Your image and likeness and called individually by You. Lord I pray today that we will all know you intimately as the only true God and Jesus Christ whom you have sent in knowledge, in conviction and in commitment. Help us all to receive this totally with our whole being by the help Your Holy Spirit in us presents. We earnestly intercede not just for ourselves but others whom You are calling into this one body of believers, that they will come to this wonderful knowledge with total conviction and total commitment.

Dear Holy Spirit, open our spiritual eyes, ears and heart to see, hear, perceive and accept each believer in Christ as one body of believers and that we will desist from segregating the bride of Christ into denominational or doctrinal lines instituted by men, but only by the fact that they know You totally as the only true and everlasting God and Jesus Christ, the Messiah, whom You have sent through the power and presence of Your self-same, one and only Holy Spirit in them and in us in Jesus name, amen

In concluding, it is difficult and almost impossible for anyone in intimate relationship with Jesus to do anything to divide His body. Hence our call for intimacy with Him. Remember the words of Apostle Paul in **Ephesians 4:1-6**

1 I, therefore, the prisoner of the Lord, beseech you to walk worthy of the calling with which you were called,2 with all lowliness and gentleness, with long-suffering, bearing with one another in love,**3 endeavoring to keep the _unity of the Spirit_ in the bond of peace.4 There is _one body and one Spirit, just as you were called in one hope of your calling; 5 one Lord, one faith, one baptism;_**

6 one God and Father of all, who is above all, and through all, and in you all.

Testimony: Amongst testimonies reaching us via our online outreach, a volunteer at a prison in Gilroy, California is now adopting the OTAKADA.org online e-discipleship portal to reach the inmates in prison. Thanks for praying, pray that the inmate will encounter Christ intimately in Jesus name.

Shalom!

Bro Monday Ogwuojo Ogbe – e-discipleship at OTAKADA.org

Chapter 3 - Pride and Disunity Go Hand in Hand

Family Prayer for unity

God made us a family.
We need one another.
We love one another.
We forgive one another.
We work together.
We play together.
We worship together.
Together we use God's word.
Together we grow in Christ.
Together we love all people.
Together we serve our God.
Together we hope for heaven.
These are our hopes and ideals.
Help us to attain them,
O God, through Jesus Christ our Lord.

Key verse:

James 4:6
But He gives more grace. Therefore He says: "God resists the proud, But gives grace to the humble."

John 17:20-23
20 I am not praying just for these followers. I am also praying for everyone else who will have faith because of

what my followers will say about me. 21 I want all of them to be one with each other, just as I am one with you and you are one with me. I also want them to be one with us. Then the people of this world will believe that you sent me.

22 I have honored my followers in the same way you honored me, in order that they may be one with each other, just as we are one. 23 I am one with them, and you are one with me, so they may become completely one. Then this world's people will know that you sent me. They will know that you love my followers as much as you love me.

Proverbs 16: 18 Too much pride will destroy you.

1 Peter 5:5
5 Likewise you younger people, submit yourselves to your elders. Yes, all of you be submissive to one another, and be clothed with humility, for "God resists the proud, But gives grace to the humble."

Ephesians 4:3-6;11-16
3 endeavoring to keep the unity of the Spirit in the bond of peace.

4 There is one body and one Spirit, just as you were called in one hope of your calling;

5 one Lord, one faith, one baptism;6 one God and Father of all, who is above all, and through all, and in you all.11 And He Himself gave some to be apostles, some prophets, some evangelists, and some pastors and teachers,12 for the equipping of the saints for the work of ministry, for the edifying of the body of Christ,13 till we all come to the unity of the faith and of the knowledge of the Son of God, to a perfect man, to the measure of the stature of the

fullness of Christ;

14 that we should no longer be children, tossed to and fro and carried about with every wind of doctrine, by the trickery of men, in the cunning craftiness of deceitful plotting,

15 but, speaking the truth in love, may grow up in all things into Him who is the head—Christ—

16 from whom the whole body, joined and knit together by what every joint supplies, according to the effective working by which every part does its share, causes growth of the body for the edifying of itself in love.

2 Timothy 2:23-26

23 But avoid foolish and ignorant disputes, knowing that they generate strife.

24 And a servant of the Lord must not quarrel but be gentle to all, able to teach, patient,

25 in humility correcting those who are in opposition, if God perhaps will grant them repentance, so that they may know the truth,

26 and that they may come to their senses and escape the snare of the devil, having been taken captive by him to do his will.

We are looking at the nexus between intercession and unity. The first series is on the issue of pride and disunity and how this undermines our intercessory effort and subsequently, our exchange for service in the vineyard.

After careful observation and much prayer, we have drawn the conclusion that at the heart of disunity in the body of Christ is deep rooted pride. Being prideful means having or showing an arrogant superiority to and disdain of that one view as unworthy. Pride can only be found where there is no love. Where there is no love, there is no God because God is love. Our love for God is the root while our love for the brethren is the fruit. Jesus says, Christian will be known by the fruit of love they manifest. The world will know us by the love we have for one another.

It is amazing that we have failed to learn from the attack going on upon the church worldwide that united we stand and divided we will certainly fall and fail. To date, Christians and indeed Christian organizations still carry on as lone Rangers right in the middle of the battlefield. We act like soldiers without commander in chief because we have no chain of commander and even when they are available, we trust no one to work with. It is either you are part of my denomination or I don't fight with you. We have made ourselves willing prey for the enemy because of deep rooted pride and affinity to organization that has no registration or recognition in scheme of heaven.

God does not see denominations neither does He see mission organization. God sees people who make up a United body of Christ. Until we see ourselves first as Christians before we are members of local Assemblies, we will continue to make ourselves willing prey before the enemy. As long as we believe our local assemblies are better than others and having all that it takes, we will continue to undermine the effectiveness of our intercessory and intervention efforts in our day and age.

God will not support disobedience. God will not give grace but will resist the proud. Come let us humble ourselves today, return to the place of unity of the spirit where grace is guaranteed so we can find help in time of need.

Prayer: Dear Lord God, we ask for your visitation to our various gathering, to our prayer closet in the secret place, speak from and to our hearts this day, put your burden for unity of spirit upon your church that we will willingly reach out to one another in love and draw resources – spiritual, human and material to meet the challenges of persecution in our midst and more importantly, that we will confront the enemy at the gates before the manifest in the physical realm as we march on, as a mighty army to fulfill the mandate of making disciples of all nations. Give us no peace until we do the needful in Jesus name, amen
shalom!

Chapter 4 - Subtle Issues That Divide Us And How To Respond

"We must love one another as God loves each one of us. To be able to love, we need a clean heart. Prayer is what gives us a clean heart. The fruit of prayer is a deepening of faith and the fruit of faith is love. The fruit of love is service, which is compassion in action" – Mother Teresa

"If we don't love one another we falsify our claim to be disciples" Pastor Thabiti Anyabwile

Key verse:

John 13:34-35 New International Version (NIV) –

A New Commandment to All Believers in Christ

34 "A new command I give you: Love one another. As I have loved you, so you must love one another. 35 By this everyone will know that you are my disciples, if you love one another."

Ephesians 4:14-16 New Living Translation (NLT) –

You don't have all that it takes, we need each other!

14 Then we will no longer be immature like children. We won't be tossed and blown about by every wind of new teaching. We will not be influenced when people try to trick us with lies so clever they sound like the

truth. 15 Instead, we will speak the truth in love, growing in every way more and more like Christ, who is the head of his body, the church. 16 He makes the whole body fit together perfectly. As each part does its own special work, it helps the other parts grow, so that the whole body is healthy and growing and full of love.

Mark 1:23-27 New Living Translation (NLT) –

The Devil is in Our church gatherings, dividing us – Beware! – Don't open yourself up to manipulation by the evil one.

23 Suddenly, a man in the synagogue who was possessed by an evil[a] spirit cried out, 24 "Why are you interfering with us, Jesus of Nazareth? Have you come to destroy us? I know who you are—the Holy One of God!"

25 But Jesus reprimanded him. "Be quiet! Come out of the man," he ordered. 26 At that, the evil spirit screamed, threw the man into a convulsion, and then came out of him.

27 Amazement gripped the audience, and they began to discuss what had happened. "What sort of new teaching is this?" they asked excitedly. "It has such authority! Even evil spirits obey his orders!"

1 Corinthians 11:28-30 New Living Translation (NLT) –

Don't be in a hurry to take communion, check yourself, it can cause, sickness and even death! Don't mess with God, God does kill Christians too! Remember Ananias and Sapphira

28 That is why you should examine yourself before eating the bread and drinking the cup. 29 For if you eat the bread or drink the cup without honoring the body of Christ,[a] you are eating and drinking God's judgment upon yourself. 30 That is why many of you are weak and sick and some have even died.

2 Corinthians 10:2-8 New Living Translation (NLT) –

Stop fighting in the physical!

2 Well, I am begging you now so that when I come I won't have to be bold with those who think we act from human motives.

3 We are human, but we don't wage war as humans do. 4 [a]We use God's mighty weapons, not worldly weapons, to knock down the strongholds of human reasoning and to destroy false arguments. 5 We destroy every proud obstacle that keeps people from knowing God. We capture their rebellious thoughts and teach them to obey Christ. 6 And after you have become fully obedient, we will punish everyone who remains disobedient.

7 Look at the obvious facts.[b] Those who say they belong to Christ must recognize that we belong to

Christ as much as they do. 8 I may seem to be boasting too much about the authority given to us by the Lord. But our authority builds you up; it doesn't tear you down. So I will not be ashamed of using my authority.

We will be looking at those subtle issues that divide us and how we should tackle them. Enjoy the reading and take decisive action to engaging other believers as part of one body in Christ today! Our disunity undermines our message to the lost. There are many that are waiting on the sidelines to see sanity in us believers, don't be seen as hindering Gods work of redemption among men.

While some divisions or disunity among Christians are obvious, others are subtler. Why does God allow it? Is it because He wants to make it hard on us? Or are the reasons as old as the church itself? Satan has always been involved in the church. It is notable that the first place Jesus cast out a demon was in the synagogue, which was Jesus' church (Mark 1:23-27).

The devil has always been at work in the church. I guess he felt if he couldn't beat them, he would just join them. His ways are subtle, so it is important to see how he has caused such division. With this in mind, let us explore the methods of this master tactician and how we can overcome his influence.

1. Inability to Understand God's Paradox

Honest people who are sincerely seeking God can come up with very different notions about the teachings in the Bible. This is because God has purposely put paradox in Scripture. He doesn't want us to approach Him through knowledge, but rather through childlike faith. It is His paradox that confounds knowledge and the wisdom of the world. Here are a few paradoxes in Scripture: law and grace; predestination and free will; one God in three; Christ as God and Christ as man; salvation by grace and work out your salvation with fear and trembling; judge not and he who is spiritual judges all things (Isaiah 55:8-9).

If I only believe in the law of God, I may become motivated by fear of God, which affects my intimacy with Him. If I only focus on grace, I may not fear the consequences of sin. Both sides of the paradox must be balanced by each other. The Corinthians received the message of grace and then began to sin with reckless abandonment. They believed they were no longer under the law. The result was death and sickness in the Corinthian church (1 Cor. 11:30). In the same way, Jesus taught us grace and love, but was unwilling to cast aside God's law (Matt 5:17-19).

Every doctrine that divides the church has paradox in it. We will begin to know the true spirit of God when we can embrace both sides of the paradox by faith. Only then can we say all things are predestined and yet I have free will to choose. Only with God is such a thing possible. We say that we believe, with God, all things are possible, but then deny that paradox is possible. Childlike faith has no problem accepting the impossible. When Christians begin to appreciate each other's viewpoints without feeling threatened, we will no longer be separated by the paradox of God; we will be united in the spirit of love.

2. Confusion of Temporal with Eternal Principles

There is much confusion over temporal and eternal truths. As I stated earlier, many Christians want to argue over a particular viewpoint in Scripture without considering the passages in paradox to that viewpoint. Because we want God to fit into our logic box, we discard any nonconforming Scripture, or simply ignore it. If we acknowledge the opposite Scriptural reference, our doctrine must be modified to accommodate both Scriptures. In the temporal, God's law is still in effect. By this I mean we have consequences by not following the law. I hear the principle of grace being preached from many pulpits, too often at the expense of the law. The grace is an eternal law that is applied to our eternal spirit, but it should not give us the idea that we can sin with no temporal affect.

In the natural, if you break the law, you will suffer the consequences. If you are speeding and you get a ticket, you might argue to the policeman that you are not under the law, but I doubt it would do any good. The eternal law of grace will keep us out of the lake of fire but will not keep us from the consequences of violating the law in the temporal. Obedience to the law doesn't save us, but it will keep us out of a whole bunch of trouble. The confusion over law and grace has caused many

Christians to be entrapped in sin and division (Romans 7:7-8).

Confusion over the temporal and eternal principles often divides the body of Christ. True wisdom comes when we can be gracious with brothers and sisters who have not yet come to a fuller understanding of the temporal and eternal truths. Jesus said to His church, "Most assuredly, I say to you, whoever commits sin is a slave of sin (John 8:34). In other words, Satan can gain great authority in our lives if we reject the commands of Christ.

3. Incorrect Motives of the Heart – 1 Cor 13:1-3

When did God ever make our relationship with Him and people about knowing all things, gifts of the Spirit, or pious acts? Too often we make fellowship too much about gifts, doctrines, good works, and sacrifice. According to the Scripture above, none of these things matter to God if they are not motivated by love. All gifts of God are wonderful, but they are not an evidence of a right heart. They should never be seen as a badge of spirituality. Even our sacrifices to God do not impress Him if we are not motivated by love.

The true mark of a Christian is not his knowledge or doctrine, but rather is the spirit of love. Satan has deceived Christians into believing that fellowship must be based on particular viewpoints and doctrines. How sad to see the division in Christianity because of differing doctrines. Too often Christians accuse one another of heresy, blasphemy and the like, thereby becoming an accuser of the brethren. We must be careful not to take on the role of accuser. This role belongs to Satan and we should always steer clear of it. If I am motivated by anger and hatred, how can I say the love of God abides in me (1 John 4:20)?

We need to understand that God is perfectly fine with differing levels of understanding. Not all children learn at the same rate or are they the same in gifts and personality. We should never be angry or hateful when a brother has been taught or experienced a differing view. There is truth in most doctrines, but perhaps the balancing paradox has been overlooked. One person may have come out of the bondage of fear and can only see the grace of God, while another may have come out of the bondage of anarchy and appreciates the discipline of law. One may focus on law while the other focuses on grace. One might be caught up in gifts while another might be focused on the Word. Why should either focus upset us? Rejoice that they have received understanding of God's truth, especially when they needed that part of the truth at a critical time in their life.

Be patient and love your brethren and perhaps they will be more attuned to what God has taught you. Both sides can be wrong if motivated incorrectly. If my focus on the law is because I'm afraid God will get me, then I am really motivated by the spirit of fear, not love. If I take advantage of grace and violate the law, I am motivated by the spirit of selfishness, which has no love in it. The subtlety of wrong motives divides the body of Christ.

4. The Religious Spirit – Luke 9:51-56

What is a religious spirit? A religious spirit is when we take the Word of God and use it to destroy others. It was the spirit of religion that found reasons to put Jesus to death though there was no evil in His actions. Too often we have been deceived into thinking we are defenders of the faith when really, we have succumbed to a religious spirit. From the Great Inquisition to an argument in Sunday school, the religious spirit disrupts and divides.

The reason Jesus rebuked the disciples is because, in one moment, they threw out the teaching of Jesus to love your enemies and those who despitefully use you. Instead they wanted to kill an entire population of people in the name of Jesus. While they thought, they were righteous, Jesus' rebuke showed them that their true motive was evil before God. Think about it—they wanted to murder everyone in the village, including women and children, in the name of God!

"When Satan spoke through Peter, Jesus sternly rebuked him as well. But He turned and said to Peter, 'Get behind Me, Satan! You are an offense to Me, for you are not mindful of the things of God, but the things of men'" (Matt 16:23). Peter had no idea that the thoughts that came into his mind were not his own. Jesus pointed out the true author of his words and would have nothing to do with them.

The religious spirit is a divider of the body of Christ. Its purpose is to cause us to be caught up in doctrines and disputes rather than yielding to the Holy Spirit of love (1 Tim 6:3-5 & James 1:12-13).

We are not approved by our knowledge of God or our doctrines; we are approved by what manner of spirit we are. Does the spirit of love rule your heart, or are you ruled by disputes and self-righteousness?

It is time for the whole body of Christ to come together to present a unified spirit of love to the world. The religious spirit is hated by the world. Even they can see it is full of hatred, murder, and condemnation. It is time in these last days to say, "I love my Catholic, Presbyterian, Baptist, Charismatic, Methodist, and Pentecostal brethren even though we are all striving to better understand the paradox in Biblical doctrine." None of us have arrived yet. We all agree Jesus is Lord and it was God who sent Him to give us life eternal. Maturity in Christ is not gauged by the knowledge of God but by the Spirit of God in us (2 Cor. 10:5).

Prayer: Dear Lord God, we pray for Your body of believers today, by the authority in Your name, we tear down every subtle walls the enemy has built up between us to divide us and re-establish the wall of love amongst us because You said, people will know we are Yours by the love we have for one another independent of institution, creed, doctrine and unspoken rules in Jesus name we have prayed with thanksgiving. Make us one Lord in Spirit, Amen.

Shalom!

Chapter 5 - Solving The Problem Of Disunity By The Corinthian's Example

"Divisions, strife, and jealousies block Christians from becoming spiritually mature. If we want to grow-up and become like Jesus, we need to learn to think like Jesus, we need to learn to think like He does and be unified in Him."

"From the first Day of Pentecost, the Holy Spirit has proven that He will only come to the degree that we have unity" – Rick Joyner

Key verse:

1 Corinthians 1:10-17

10. Now I am calling you over, brothers,
on account of the name of our Lord Jesus Christ,
in order that you might keep speaking the same thing
and that there might not continue to be divisions among you,
but that you might be mended
through [having] the same mind
and through [having] the same opinion.
11. for it has been shown to me
concerning you, my brothers,
by the men from Chloe,
that quarrels continue to exist among you.
12. Now [what] I'm saying is this: that each of you are saying,
"As for me, I am of Paul,"

and, "As for me, I am of Apollos,"
and, "As for me, I am of Cephas,"
and, "As for me I am of Christ!"
13. Christ has been divided!
It wasn't Paul who was crucified for you,
neither were was it into the name of Paul that you
were baptized!
14. I'm thankful to God that I baptized none of you
except Crispus and Gaius,
15. in order that no one might say that you were
baptized into MY name.
16. Now I did also baptize the household of
Stephanus.
As for the rest, I don't know if I baptized anyone
else.
17. For Christ did not commission me to baptize, but
rather to evangelize –
[and that] not by sophistication of words,
so that the cross of Christ would not be nullified.

Some Illustration to reflect on:

Tuning fork:

A.W. Tozer, "Has it ever occurred to you that one
hundred pianos all tuned to the same fork are
automatically tuned to each other? They are of one
accord by being tuned, not to each other, but to another
standard to which each one must individually bow. So
one hundred worshippers together, each one looking
away to Christ, are in heart nearer to each other than
they could possibly be were they to be come 'unity'

conscious and turn their eyes away from God to strive for closer fellowship." (*The Pursuit of God*)

1. The Problem – introduction:
   Situation in Corinth
2. The church in Corinth was divided over a lot of issues:
   - They were arguing about whether or not Christians could eat meat offered to idols,
   - They were arguing about whether or not Christians could marry,
   - They were showing off with spiritual gifts in order to prove that some were more spiritual than others,
   - People were interrupting public worship by disorderly conduct,
   - They were aligning themselves behind one Christian leader and criticizing the rest of the people in the congregation who were aligned with a different Christian leader,
   - They had a feminist group vying for power,
   - Even during communion, they were dividing into rich people at one table and poor people at another,
   - and Christians were suing each other in the public courts.
3. Since Paul had planted the church in Corinth, he had kept tabs on the church:
   - Paul seems to have paid a second visit to Corinth before writing his epistle, For in 2 Cor. 12:4; 2Cor. 13:1-2, he speaks of his intention of paying them a third visit, implying he had already twice visited them.

- During his three years' stay at Ephesus he could have easily hired one of the many ships that travelled between Ephesus and Corinth and revisited his Corinthian converts.
- This second visit was probably a short one (compare 1 Cor. 16:7); and was probably painful and humiliating to Paul as he saw (2 Cor. 2:1; 2 Cor. 12:21), the scandalous conduct of so many of his own converts. (JFB)
- Apollos had gone to Corinth with letters of commendation from Priscilla and Aquila (Acts 18:28-19:1), but apparently left because of factions in that church (1 Cor. 1:10-12) and returned to Ephesus. When Paul urged Apollos to go back, he declined (1 Cor. 16:12).
- Paul then sent Timothy over to Corinth to put an end to the factions (1 Cor. 4:17), but the outcome was uncertain (1 Cor. 16:10.)...
- Some of the household of Chloe who were familiar with the situation in Corinth had also brought word to Paul in Ephesus (1 Cor. 16:5-7)
- The church in Corinth also had sent a committee(Stephanas, Fortunatus, Achaicus) to Paul in Ephesus.
- And Paul had also already writtena brief first letter to the Corinthians directing them "not to associate with fornicators." (1Cor. 5:9-12) That letter probably also mentioned the fund-raiser he was organizing for the poor in Jerusalem (1Cor. 16:2) So 1st Cor. is actually Paul's 2nd letter to them.

4. **Verse 12 mentions 4 factions in Corinth: For the most part we can only guess:**
"I am of Paul" party:

- May have been people converted under Paul's ministry
- Perhaps baptized by Paul
- Probably liked systematic theology because that's how Paul taught
- Probably also were hard-core about the Gospel for Gentiles
- Paul also had refused to be supported by a patron, but rather worked for his living at Corinth, so he may have been the blue-collar working-man's apostle of choice

Apollos Party:
- From Alexandria, Egypt – maybe black.
- Came after Paul and baptized people. "I planted, Apollos watered" (3:6).
- Preferred his teaching style – philosophical, rhetorical, eloquent.
- Maybe like a Barak Obama.

Cephas Party:
- Aramaic for Peter (Jn. 1:42).
- The "real" apostle.
- Probably name-droppers, not representative of Peter himself.
- Probably Judaizers (Gal 2:11-14), who insisted that Gentile converts get circumcised and follow Jewish food laws and customs.

Christ Party:
- Perhaps they weren't willing to submit to any of the apostles.
- Perhaps they thought they could hear straight from God and didn't need the Bible.

- Perhaps like the Christian Church of today, they got fed up with everybody's denominationalism and conflicting creeds and tried to form a non-denomination which had "no creed but Christ" and turned into just another denomination.

5. Archaeology and house church size in Corinth

- Some amount of splitting up would have been natural in a home-based church.
- Romans 16:23 – Gaius's house was where the church in Corinth initially met.
- Thistleton cites archaeological evidence that churches in that era tended to break up and meet in two different homes once they got up to 40 people in attendance.
- Dividing into multiple meeting places because no one place is big enough for everybody to meet is fine.
- There may even be cultural reasons to preserve and enjoy different historical worship traditions.
- But splitting over schools of orthodox doctrine or splitting over interpersonal conflict was not o.k. in Paul's book.

6. Clement testified to continued divisions in Corinth in 95AD

- First Epistle starts, "The Church of God which sojourns at Rome, to the Church of God sojourning at Corinth, to them that are called and sanctified by the will of God, through our Lord Jesus Christ: Grace unto you, and peace, from Almighty God through Jesus Christ, be multiplied.

- ...we feel that we have been somewhat tardy in turning our attention to the points respecting which you consulted us; and especially to that shameful and detestable sedition, utterly abhorrent to the elect of God, which a few rash and self-confident persons have kindled to such a pitch of frenzy, that your venerable and illustrious name, worthy to be universally loved, has suffered grievous injury...

- (Chapter 45) Ye are fond of contention, brethren, and full of zeal about things which do not pertain to salvation. Look carefully into the Scriptures, which are the true utterances of the Holy Spirit... Why are there strives, and tumults, and divisions, and schisms, and wars among you? Have we not [all] one God and one Christ? Is there not one Spirit of grace poured out upon us? And have we not one calling in Christ? Why do we divide and tear to pieces the members of Christ, and raise up strife against our own body, and have reached such a height of madness as to forget that "we are members one of another?" Remember the words of our Lord Jesus Christ, how He said, "Woe to that man [by whom offences come]! It were better for him that he had never been born, than that he should cast a stumbling-block before one of my elect. Yea, it were better for him that a millstone should be hung about [his neck], and he should be sunk in the depths of the sea, than that he should cast a stumbling-block before one of my little ones." Your schism has subverted [the faith of] many, has discouraged many, has given rise to doubt in many, and has caused grief to us all...

- Take up the epistle of the blessed Apostle Paul. What did he write to you at the time when the

Gospel first began to be preached? Truly, under the inspiration of the Spirit, he wrote to you concerning himself, and Cephas, and Apollos, because even then parties had been formed among you. But that inclination for one above another entailed less guilt upon you, inasmuch as your partialities were then shown towards apostles, already of high reputation, and towards a man whom they had approved. But now reflect who those are that have perverted you, and lessened the renown of your far-famed brotherly love. It is disgraceful, beloved, yea, highly disgraceful, and unworthy of your Christian profession, that such a thing should be heard of as that the most steadfast and ancient Church of the Corinthians should, on account of one or two persons, engage in sedition against its presbyters. And this rumor has reached not only us, but those also who are unconnected with us; so that, through your infatuation, the name of the Lord is blasphemed, while danger is also brought upon yourselves.

- (Chapter XLVIII.) Let us therefore, with all haste, put an end to this [state of things]; and let us fall down before the Lord, and beseech Him with tears, that He would mercifully be reconciled to us, and restore us to our former seemly and holy practice of brotherly love... Let a man be faithful: let him be powerful in the utterance of knowledge; let him be wise in judging of words; let him be pure in all his deeds; yet the more he seems to be superior to others [in these respects], the more humble-minded ought he to be, and to seek the common good of all, and not merely his own advantage.

We see here some of the solutions proposed by Clement of Rome, a godly man a generation after Paul, but let us look at what Paul himself writes in I Cor. 1 about the solution to this problem:

God's solution:

1. **Fight against church splits by maintaining a unified front and working to be mended in the same thinking patterns.**
   The father of Alexander the Great perfected a fighting technique that made the Macedonian army almost invincible. It has been nicknamed the "Turtle" formation, because the soldiers would form patterns where everyone's shield was positioned facing the enemy so that the whole army was covered by a "shell" and not vulnerable to arrows.

   - Imagine what would have happened, however, if two soldiers were to get mad at each other and turn their spears and shields to face each other? They would then become vulnerable to the enemy's arrows because their shields wouldn't be facing the enemy anymore. As Christians, we need to maintain a unified front so that we don't get taken out by our own in-fighting.
   Paul's words in v.10 are literally "keep speaking the same thing" rendered "agree" in the modern English versions.

2. **Paul uses a term for mending fishing nets** (Mt. 4:21) toward the end of v.10 – translated "perfectly joined together/united/made complete" in some versions. The word means "to put in order, restore to former condition" .

3. How do we get this restoration?
- By being of the "same mind and same judgment/opinion/purpose/intention/thought."
- This means that Christian unity is a thinkingunity, not a mindless ecumenism.
- We achieve that unity by studying the same Bibletogether and coming to the same conclusions on the major issues together. It is unity in knowing sound doctrine.
- Calvin explains that the "same mind" means having the same faith in God, and "judgment" means having a will to loveyour brother.
4. God's Call to unity in:
- John 17 – Jesus prayed that His people would be one as He is one with God.
- Eph 4 – One lord, one faith, one baptism
- Phil 2 – have this mind in yourselves which was also in Christ...cross

1. **Solution #1: Maintaining a unified front** and growing together in the same Biblical thinking patterns.
2. **Keep Christ central rather than yourself.**
3. ILLUSTRATION: Tuning fork: A.W. Tozer, "Has it ever occurred to you that one hundred pianos all tuned to the same fork are automatically tuned to each other? They are of one accord by being tuned, not to each other, but to another standard to which each one must individually bow. So one hundred worshippers together, each one looking away to Christ, are in heart nearer to each other than they could possibly be were they to be come 'unity' conscious and turn their eyes away from

God to strive for closer fellowship." (*The Pursuit of God*)

4. **v.10 "I exhort/beseech/appeal** to you by the name of our Lord Jesus Christ"
5. **v.13 – "Is Christ divided?"**
- Absurdity of a cutting Jesus in half and the two halves doing different things
- "We murder, to dissect" – William Wordsworth
6. **"Was Paul crucified for you?"**
- By this bit of humor, Paul puts the focus back on the centrality of Christ
- We were redeemed by Christ in His death. When you were baptized into Christ, you were enlisted under his banner and will never have any other spiritual lord.
7. **"Were you baptized in the name of Paul?"**
- Baptism was to be in the name of the Father, Son, and Holy Spirit – Mt. 28:18ff – not anyone else.
- It doesn't matter who baptized you. It doesn't matter if that person was a fake Christian who left the church later. What matters is that you received the sign and seal of your covenantal relationship with God.
8. **"Jesus is enough**. He is substantive enough to be the basis of your unity... If [you] would be Christ-centered instead of people-centered or issues-centered, disunity will take care of itself."
9. **Preach the cross rather than getting involved in intellectual rabbit-trails.**
10. **Don't get off on the rabbit trail of baptism.** Keep the cross central. Some of us were immersed, some were effused, some were sprinkled. Some here were baptized as infants, others as adults. It's over now; don't get worked up over whether you got

wet the "right" way. The Bible doesn't teach us to make issue of how you were baptized. Christ's work on the cross is what saves you, not your baptism.

11. **(v.17)** "not with sophistication/wisdom/cleverness/eloquence of words/speech lest the cross of Christ be made of none effect/void/nullified/emptied."

- Calvin: "No effect if... just eloquence and show... the teaching of the gospel... should savor of the nature of the cross... despised and contemptible rather than glorious in the eyes of the world... The ... Corinthians were tickled with a silly fondness for high-sounding style, hence they needed... to be brought back to the abasement of the cross... the gospel in its simplicity without false ornament."
- In Corinth, the cosmopolitan merchants were using Christianity as a way to gain social status. This has been a problem throughout history.
- Today, missionary friends in majority-world countries have told us that most seekers want to become Christians so that they can move to wealthy nations and get wealthy. It's a constant struggle to explain to people who come with worldly motives that becoming a Christian is about being a follower of Jesus. It's about the way of the cross.

12. **Identify your unique calling and stick to it.**
"I was not sent to Baptize but to Evangelize" v.17
Paul's commission in Acts 9:15 does not mention baptism.

- The chief thing for Paul was to make Jesus known to "Gentiles, kings, and the Children of Israel"

- Doesn't mean he repudiated baptism – Paul obviously baptized Crispus (the former president of the synagogue in Corinth) and Gaius and everybody in Stephanas' house
- (and, by the way, I Tim. 3:4 says that Paul considered a man's children to be part of his house.)

13. **Exposure of public to gospel is the first step**, the apostolic calling. Church development happens after that – that's apparently what Apollos was good at.

14. **What is your calling in life?**
- What have I noticed in the Bible that God commands me to do?
- What do I love to do?
- What do Godly counselors urge me to focus on?
- What opportunities has God opened up for me already to do?
- When these things line up, you can be confident that you have a calling.

15. **Once you are clear on your calling**, don't get distracted from it. Keep it front and center. This will help the church stay unified.

Jesus is another great example of this kind of focus on calling. His calling was to save the world (John 12:47). He was perfectly capable of judging the world and being a great king, but He didn't take that path when He was sure that His father wanted him to save the world through dying on the cross. While Jesus was suffering for our sins on the cross, He could have called a thousand angels to rescue him and kill all the bad guys, but He didn't because

He knew He needed to stick to His calling. Without His death there would be no church to call into unity.

Follow Christ's example. Stick to your calling. Preach the cross. Get yourself out of the way and keep Christ central. And present a united front with your fellow believers by working to be of the same mind. And by God's grace, this church will not break apart.

Prayer: Dear Lord God, visit us today. Cause us to focus on You and what You stand for. Help us to take attention off ourselves and let it rest on You. Help us to keep You central in everything that we do while allowing channels of engagement with our brothers and sisters in the faith despite our deferring styles and method of worship. You have a purpose and plan for every one of us that fits perfectly into Your grand plan. Open our spiritual eyes Lord to see and to pursue this without distractions and help us to present a unified front with our fellow believers always to the glory, honor and adoration of Your name, in Jesus name we have prayed with thanksgiving

Shalom

Chapter 6 - Disagreement and Division over Lifestyle differences between Younger and Older believers – How do you handle it? Criticism

Introduction

Dealing with division in churches especially between the older and younger believers in Christ over differences in lifestyle and how these breeds toxic criticism amongst the brethren that causes division within and between churches and how best to handle it. Issues like day of worship, what one eats or drinks, how one keeps the hair or dresses has divided churches. Let us look at what Jesus and Paul has to say about these in scriptures below to help provide core content relevant to this challenge and how these issues were dealt with then and how we can apply them now to foster unity in the body of Christ.

Key verse:

MATTHEW 7:3-5 THE MESSAGE (MSG)

A SIMPLE GUIDE FOR BEHAVIOR

7 1-5 "Don't pick on people, jump on their failures, criticize their faults— unless, of course, you want the same treatment. That critical spirit has a way of boomeranging. It's easy to see a smudge on your neighbor's face and be oblivious to the ugly sneer on your own. Do you have the nerve to say, 'Let me wash your face for you,' when your own face is distorted by contempt? It's this whole traveling road-show mentality all over again, playing a holier-than-thou part instead of just living your part. Wipe

that ugly sneer off your own face, and you might be fit to offer a washcloth to your neighbor

ROMANS 14:1- THE MESSAGE (MSG)
CULTIVATING GOOD RELATIONSHIPS

14 Welcome with open arms fellow believers who don't see things the way you do. And don't jump all over them every time they do or say something you don't agree with—even when it seems that they are strong on opinions but weak in the faith department. Remember, they have their own history to deal with. Treat them gently.

2-4 For instance, a person who has been around for a while might well be convinced that he can eat anything on the table, while another, with a different background, might assume he should only be a vegetarian and eat accordingly. But since both are guests at Christ's table, wouldn't it be terribly rude if they fell to criticizing what the other ate or didn't eat? God, after all, invited them both to the table. Do you have any business crossing people off the guest list or interfering with God's welcome? If there are corrections to be made or manners to be learned, God can handle that without your help.

5 Or, say, one person thinks that some days should be set aside as holy and another thinks that each day is pretty much like any other. There are good reasons either way. So, each person is free to follow the convictions of conscience.

6-9 What's important in all this is that if you keep a holy day, keep it for *God's* sake; if you eat meat, eat it to the glory of God and thank God for prime rib; if you're a vegetarian, eat vegetables to the glory of God and thank God for broccoli. None of us are permitted to insist on our own way in these matters. It's *God* we are answerable to—

all the way from life to death and everything in between—not each other. That's why Jesus lived and died and then lived again: so that he could be our Master across the entire range of life and death, and free us from the petty tyrannies of each other.

10-12 So where does that leave you when you criticize a brother? And where does that leave you when you condescend to a sister? I'd say it leaves you looking pretty silly—or worse. Eventually, we're all going to end up kneeling side by side in the place of judgment, facing God. Your critical and condescending ways aren't going to improve your position there one bit. Read it for yourself in Scripture:

"As I live and breathe," God says,
    "every knee will bow before me;
Every tongue will tell the honest truth
    that I and only I am God."

So tend to your knitting. You've got your hands full just taking care of your own life before God.

13-14 Forget about deciding what's right for each other. Here's what you need to be concerned about: that you don't get in the way of someone else, making life more difficult than it already is. I'm convinced—Jesus convinced me!—that everything as it is in itself is holy. We, of course, by the way we treat it or talk about it, can contaminate it.

15-16 If you confuse others by making a big issue over what they eat or don't eat, you're no longer a companion with them in love, are you? These, remember, are persons for whom Christ died. Would you risk sending them to hell over an item in their diet? Don't you dare let a piece of God-blessed food become an occasion of soul-poisoning!

17-18 God's kingdom isn't a matter of what you put in your stomach, for goodness' sake. It's what God does with your life as he sets it right, puts it together, and completes it with joy. Your task is to single-mindedly serve Christ. Do that and you'll kill two birds with one stone: pleasing the God above you and proving your worth to the people around you.

19-21 So let's agree to use all our energy in getting along with each other. Help others with encouraging words; don't drag them down by finding fault. You're certainly not going to permit an argument over what is served or not served at supper to wreck God's work among you, are you? I said it before and I'll say it again: All food is good, but it can turn bad if you use it badly, if you use it to trip others up and send them sprawling. When you sit down to a meal, your primary concern should not be to feed your own face but to share the life of Jesus. So be sensitive and courteous to the others who are eating. Don't eat or say or do things that might interfere with the free exchange of love.

22-23 Cultivate your own relationship with God, but don't impose it on others. You're fortunate if your behavior and your belief are coherent. But if you're not sure, if you notice that you are acting in ways inconsistent with what you believe—some days trying to impose your opinions on others, other days just trying to please them—then you know that you're out of line. If the way you live isn't consistent with what you believe, then it's wrong.

Conclusion

Divisions in churches often occur when disagreements over lifestyle issues grow into major arguments and church splits. Paul warned the church not to pass judgement on younger believers whose faith is still young and growing. The kingdom of God is about goodness, peace and joy in the Holy Ghost. Anything outside this is of the evil one.

Jesus went on to emphasis the importance of assessing our own stand, confirm that we are standing before we are qualified to point at other's faults and failings. What we eat, what we wear, how we dress, where and when we worship should not divide us.

Prayer

Dear Lord God, thank You for the simplicity in walking with You. Help us to be led by Your Spirit always and not to be a stumbling block to others in the race of faith. Your Spirit is love, joy and goodness. Cause us to do an internal audit of ourselves continually so we can stand blameless before you. Help us to open ourselves and welcome all who names the name of Christ and extend the heart of love in Jesus name we have prayed with thanksgiving.

DECLARATION

By authority in the name of Jesus Christ, I speak to every raging storm in the lives of those who are reading this book today, I join my faith with theirs, be it in relationships, health and finance, we proclaim peace be still, be healed and be restored in Jesus name we have declared with thanksgiving

Shalom!

Chapter 7 - Digging Deeper into the uncompromising Gospel of the Kingdom of God – Don't allow division to cause you to settle for crumps when you can have a full course meal

Introduction

"Churches and ministries that don't preach the gospel of the kingdom produce a complacent Christianity. They make no room for the supernatural, and they do not believe that all things are possible with God. This is precisely why we do not see the manifestations of God's power in the church which is the evidence that God is at work in our midst"

We will drill down the various versions of the gospel message out there and how the bible explains what the gospel of the kingdom of God really is with the intent that it will help us discern, engage and intercede for the misled brethren. We have put together **five (5) versions of the gospel messages** that does not pane out with the true gospel message and how we should handle them.

Let us start with the bible… **20 bible references** provided hereunder for your reading and meditation to help drill the message home…

Key verses:

Galatians 1:9 – If anyone preaches any gospel to you than what was you have received, let him be accursed.

Matthew 4:23 New King James Version
And Jesus went about all Galilee, teaching in their synagogues, preaching the gospel of the kingdom, and healing all kinds of sickness and all kinds of disease among the people.

Luke 4:43 Contemporary English Version

But Jesus said, "People in other towns must hear the good news about God's kingdom. This is why I was sent."

Act 10:38
How God anointed Jesus of Nazareth with the Holy Ghost and with power: who went about doing good, and healing all that were oppressed of the devil; for God was with him

Matthew 12:28
But if I cast out demons by the Spirit of God, surely the kingdom of God has come upon you.

Matthew 6:33
But seek first the kingdom of God and His righteousness, and all these things shall be added to you

Matthew 19:24
And again I say to you, it is easier for a camel to go through the eye of the needle than for a rich man to enter the kingdom of God

Matthew 21:43

Therefore I say to you, the kingdom of God will be taken from you and given to a nation bearing the fruits if it.

Matthew 24:14 New King James Version
And this gospel of the kingdom will be preached in all the world as a witness to all the nations, and then the end will come

Mark 4:10-12,26-32
10-12 When they were off by themselves, those who were close to him, along with the Twelve, asked about the stories. He told them, "You've been given insight into God's kingdom—you know how it works. But to those who can't see it yet, everything comes in stories, creating readiness, nudging them toward receptive insight. These are people—
Whose eyes are open but don't see a thing,
Whose ears are open but don't understand a word,
Who avoid making an about-face and getting forgiven."

26-29 Then Jesus said, "God's kingdom is like seed thrown on a field by a man who then goes to bed and forgets about it. The seed sprouts and grows—he has no idea how it happens. The earth does it all without his help: first a green stem of grass, then a bud, then the ripened grain. When the grain is fully formed, he reaps—harvest time!
30-32 "How can we picture God's kingdom? What kind of story can we use? It's like a pine nut. When it lands on the ground it is quite small as seeds go, yet once it is planted it grows into a huge pine tree with thick branches. Eagles nest in it."

26 And He said, "The kingdom of God is as if a man should [f]scatter seed on the ground,27 and should sleep by

night and rise by day, and the seed should sprout
and grow, he himself does not know how. [28] For the
earth yields crops by itself: first the blade, then the head,
after that the full grain in the head. [29] But when the grain
ripens, immediately he puts in the sickle, because the
harvest has come."
The Parable of the Mustard Seed

[30] Then He said, "To what shall we liken the kingdom of
God? Or with what parable shall we picture it? [31] *It is* like a
mustard seed which, when it is sown on the ground, is
smaller than all the seeds on earth; [32] but when it is sown,
it grows up and becomes greater than all herbs, and
shoots out large branches, so that the birds of the air may
nest under its shade."

Acts 1:3,7
To whom He also presented Himself alive after His
suffering by many infallible proofs, being seen by them
during forty days and speaking of things pertaining to the
kingdom of God.7 But you shall receive power when the
Holy Spirit has come upon you; and you shall be witnesses
to Me in Jerusalem, and in all Judea and Samaria, and to
the ends of the earth.

Mark 16:15-18

And He said to them, "God into all the world and preach
the gospel to every creature. He who believes and is
baptized will be saved: but he who does not believe will be
condemned. And these signs will follow those who believe;

In My name they will cast out demons; they will speak with new tongues; they will take up serpents; and if they drink anything deadly, it will by no means hurt them; they will lay hands on the sick, and they will recover."

Galatians 5:19-24 The Message (MSG)

[19-21] It is obvious what kind of life develops out of trying to get your own way all the time: repetitive, loveless, cheap sex; a stinking accumulation of mental and emotional garbage; frenzied and joyless grabs for happiness; trinket gods; magic-show religion; paranoid loneliness; cutthroat competition; all-consuming-yet-never-satisfied wants; a brutal temper; an impotence to love or be loved; divided homes and divided lives; small-minded and lopsided pursuits; the vicious habit of depersonalizing everyone into a rival; uncontrolled and uncontrollable addictions; ugly parodies of community. I could go on.

This isn't the first time I have warned you, you know. If you use your freedom this way, you will not inherit God's kingdom.

[22-23] But what happens when we live God's way? He brings gifts into our lives, much the same way that fruit appears in an orchard—things like affection for others, exuberance about life, serenity. We develop a willingness to stick with things, a sense of compassion in the heart, and a conviction that a basic holiness permeates things and people. We find ourselves involved in loyal commitments, not needing to force our way in life, able to marshal and direct our energies wisely.

[23-24] Legalism is helpless in bringing this about; it only gets in the way. Among those who belong to Christ, everything connected with getting our own way and mindlessly responding to what everyone else calls necessities is killed off for good—crucified.

Romans 14:17

[17] For the Kingdom of God is not a matter of what we eat or drink, but of living a life of goodness and peace and joy in the Holy Spirit.

1 John 3:8

He who sins is of the devil, for the devil has sinned from the beginning. For this purpose the Son of God was manifested, that He might destroy the works of the devil.

Luke 10:5-11,16

But whatever house you enter, first say, 'Peace to this house.' And if a son of peace is there, your peace will rest on it; if not it will return to you. And remain in the same house, eating and drinking such things as they give, for the labourer is worthy of his wages. Do not go from house to house. Whatever city you enter, and they receive you, eat such things as are set before you. And heal the sick there, and say to them, **'the kingdom of God has come near to you.'**

But whatever city you enter, and they do not receive you, go out into its streets and say, 'The very dust of your city which clings to us we wipe off against you. Nevertheless know this, that the kingdom of God has come near you.' 16 He who hears you hears Me, he who rejects you rejects Me, and he who rejects Me rejects Him who sent Me.

John 6:28-29,33,35,51

Then they said to Him, "What shall we do, that we may work the works of God?" 29 Jesus answered and said to them, "This is the work of God, that you believe in Him whom He sent." 33 For the bread of God is He who comes down from heaven and gives life to the world."35 And Jesus said to them, "I am the bread of life. He who comes to Me shall never hunger, and he comes to Me shall never thirst. 51I am the living bread which came down from heaven. If anyone eats of this bread, he will live forever; and the bread that I shall give is My flesh, which I shall give for the life of the world."

Matthew 6:9,10
In this manner, therefore, pray: Our Father in heaven, Hallowed be Your name. Your kingdom come. Your will be done on earth as it is in heaven.

Matthew 7:15-16
Beware of false prophets, who come to you in sheep's clothing, but inwardly they are ravenous wolves. You will know them by their fruits. Do men gather grapes from thornbushes or figs from thistles?

Continued...
Many religions have their own "gospels," and they announce good things. However, they lack supernatural power to deal with people's sin and rebelliousness and to transform their lives. They lack the power to heal a sickness or to deliver someone from mental or emotional oppressions. They are substitutes for the true gospel. Even in much of the church, parts of the gospel message have been diluted or abridged into various human versions that lack power.

In some cases, these human versions are even anti-power. The message of the gospel of the kingdom is not being presented as it was by Jesus and the early church. These significant elements have been left out: A call to wholehearted repentance and manifestation of God's presence by healing, signs, wonders, the casting out of demons, and the raising of the dead. As a result, the church has become accustomed to hearing an incomplete gospel..

Paul said in Galatians 1:9 – If anyone preaches any gospel to you than what was you have received, let him be accursed. As we call believers to unity, it is imperative that we all work from the same biblical perspective. God wants to restore the true gospel in the church, so that the good news can be preached to the world as it ought to be. Let us look closely at what we have out there.

1. The Historical Gospel

Many Christians of various denominations are fixed in a historical, traditional gospel that lacks the presence and power of God They believe in a God of history but not in a God who is with us today – a God whose name is in the present tense: "I am who I am". IF we can't bring Jesus to the here and now, then His death, resurrection, and ascension to the throne at the Father's right hand in heaven have no meaning or purpose for our present circumstances.

2. The "Future" Gospel

The mentality of much of the modern church is to present a gospel that simply proclaims forgiveness of sin so that a person can go to heaven when he or she dies. Although that is certainly part of the good news, it is not the whole gospel of the kingdom. It says nothing of reigning with Christ on earth now with dominion authority and power. Other believers reflect a different aspect of the future gospel. They believe that God can bring healing and deliverance to the people on earth. Nonetheless, since their mind-set is always that God "will" do these things, they never receive or minister them. For example, they may say, "I believe that God will heal, deliver, prosper and bring revival at some point." In other words, it will happen later, at an unspecified time in the future. Yet God is the God of the now. It is true that He acts according to His sovereignty. However, these believers keep waiting for something that God has already promised and that Jesus has already provided through His death and resurrection

3. The Social Gospel

While the "future" gospel focuses on heaven, the social gospel centers exclusively on the earth; its advocates seek to relieve societal problems, such as hunger, poverty, and injustice. Addressing people's physical needs and concerns is central to kingdom living, because God wants us to love others as He loves us. However, they often downplay or ignore the spiritual element of a relationship with God the Father through Jesus His Son. They do not seek or rely on God's supernatural power, through which people can be healed physically, emotionally, and mentally, and through which they have access to God's abundant provision, power and strength. Therefore, they do not present the complete gospel.

4. The Gospel of Conformity

This human "gospel" leaves people in a spiritual stagnant condition, unable to move forward, retaining their sin and never regaining their authority in Christ. It neither deals with the rot of rebellion nor challenges people to change, so that they are left in sickness, scarcity, and oppression. A gospel that doesn't produce change is contrary to the kingdom message of repentance that Jesus preached, and it fails to bring about the transformation that Paul urged believers to actively seek.

5. The Motivational and or Prosperity Gospel

This is a "self-help" gospel in which God's Word is spoken without power; the cross and the resurrection of Jesus are not proclaimed, and the supernatural is absent. It is a gospel adapted to what people want to hear, and it fails to confront them with the destructiveness of their sin, in an effort to avoid offending them. Its main purpose is for people to walk away feeling satisfied with themselves and encouraged to reach their personal goals. While it is good to have goals and to accomplish them, Jesus came to announce much more than that. **(Matthew 6:33)**
The gospel of the kingdom lovingly confronts us with our iniquity and challenges us to live in holiness through the resurrection life of Jesus and the power of the Holy Spirit. Jesus message does not leave us comfortable in our sinful nature.

The other version of the motivational gospel is the prosperity gospel. Please understand that God promises prosperity, and He wants to give us His provision and abundance but if all we think about is money and material goods, forgetting holiness, prayer, and serving others, then we have put the cart in front of the us.

CONCLUSION:

In concluding, churches and ministries that don't preach the gospel of the kingdom produce a complacent Christianity. They make no room for the supernatural, and they do not believe that all things are possible with God. This is precisely why we do not see the manifestations of God's power in the church which is the evidence that God is at work in our midst.

As we engage with our brothers and sisters in small groups, fellowships and churches, we need to discern the type of gospel at play. We need to lovingly point out these issues while praying for our brethren that the veil be removed from their eyes that they will walk in ALL that Christ came to give us all and proclaim aright to the world around us. But to abandon and not engage with other believers is folly and recipe for disaster waiting or already happening in our midst.

We travel the whole world to get a convert and make them sons and daughters if the devil. Jesus's rebuke to the scribes and Pharisees apply nicely here.. **Matthew 23:15–** "Woe to you, scribes and Pharisees, hypocrites! For you travel land and sea to win one proselyte, and when he is won, you make him twice as much a son of hell as yourselves... Message says – "You're hopeless, you religion scholars and Pharisees! Frauds! You go halfway around the world to make a convert, but once you get him, you make into a replica of yourselves, double-damned.

Prayer

Our heavenly Father, as we seek the unity of the Spirit amongst the brethren, open our eyes to discern the wolves in sheep's clothing amongst us as in **Matthew 7:15 Luke 10:3**. We ask that You expose them for who they really are. If they are unrepentant, we as that You silence them for Your name and Your work sake. Grant unto us boldness and courage to confront and to pray for our misled brethren to amend their ways. As we humble ourselves and are willing to learn from you, help us to stay through to the authentic gospel message to the very end. As many that seek the manifestation of Your power and presence to heal and deliver, Lord visit them today, give them the revelation of You. Heal the sick, provide for those who lack and bring comfort to the brokenhearted in Jesus name we have prayed with thanksgiving.

Shalom!

Monday Ogwuojo Ogbe – E-discipleship at Otakada.org

Chapter 8 - Compete Or Complement – Which Side Are You? The World Says Compete, God Says Complement – Team Work – Language Of Unity

"We are one in the spirit, we are one in the Lord"

Introduction

"God is calling us to complement one another not to compete with one another. He is calling us to unity in diversity and not uniformity. Our heavenly Father is calling us to operate in our office, where we have strength and ask for help from others who have strength we don't have. Asking us to reach out to one another for the work of ministry. He is aware of the fact that we can do all things through Christ who strengthens us but He knows we are not expert in everything. God is asking us to observe how He operates so we can operate the way He operates."

The Father, the Son and the Holy Spirit are one. The Father is not The Son, The Son is not the Holy Spirit, yet they operate and function as one. The Body is not the Spirit, or is the Spirit the mind but in this part of eternity, all three must work together so we can be a complete human being. The man is not the woman, neither is the woman the man but God said, they are one. **God is interested in who we are and also interested in what we do with who we are.**

Let us dig into the scriptures and see team work at play in the operation and dealing of our heavenly Father so that we can begin to earnestly reach out to our other brothers and sister in different Christian groups, fellowships, churches and mission organizations to equip each other to do the work of ministry He has called all of us to so that we can reach out to the lost in a very effective and efficient way thereby speeding up His return and then the end will come..

Key Verses

Genesis 1: 1,2,26,27
1 In the beginning God created the heavens and the earth.[a] **2** The earth was formless and empty, and darkness covered the deep waters. **And the Spirit of God was hovering over the surface of the waters.**

26 Then God said, **"Let us make human beings[b] in our image, to be like us.**They will reign over the fish in the sea, the birds in the sky, the livestock, all the wild animals on the earth,[c] and the small animals that scurry along the ground."

27 So God created human beings[d] in his own image. In the image of God he created them; male and female he created them.

Genesis 2:18
18 Then the Lord God said, "It is not good for the man to be alone. **I will make a helper who is just right for him."**

²⁴ This explains why a man leaves his father and mother and is joined to his wife, **and the two are united into one.**

John 10:30 New Living Translation (NLT)
³⁰ **The Father and I are one."**

Matthew 19:5 New Living Translation (NLT)
⁵ And he said, **"'This explains why a man leaves his father and mother and is joined to his wife, and the two are united into one.**

John 14: 8-17
⁸ Philip said, "Lord, show us the Father, and we will be satisfied."
⁹ Jesus replied, "Have I been with you all this time, Philip, and yet you still don't know who I am? Anyone who has seen me has seen the Father! So why are you asking me to show him to you? ¹⁰ Don't you believe that I am in the Father and the Father is in me? The words I speak are not my own, but my Father who lives in me does his work through me. ¹¹ Just believe that I am in the Father and the Father is in me. Or at least believe because of the work you have seen me do.

¹² "I tell you the truth, anyone who believes in me will do the same works I have done, and even greater works, because I am going to be with the Father. ¹³ You can ask for anything in my name, and I will do it, so that the Son can bring glory to the Father. ¹⁴ Yes, ask me for anything in my name, and I will do it!

¹⁵ **"If you love me, obey[d] my commandments. ¹⁶ And I will ask the Father, and he will give you another Advocate,[e] who will never leave you. ¹⁷ He is the Holy**

Spirit, who leads into all truth. The world cannot receive him, because it isn't looking for him and doesn't recognize him. But you know him, because he lives with you now and later will be in you.[f]

John 17:21 New Living Translation (NLT)
[21] I pray that they will all be one, just as you and I are one—as you are in me, Father, and I am in you. And may they be in us so that the world will believe you sent me.

1 Corinthians 12 New Living Translation (NLT)

12 Now, dear brothers and sisters,[a] regarding your question about the special abilities the Spirit gives us. I don't want you to misunderstand this. [2] You know that when you were still pagans, you were led astray and swept along in worshiping speechless idols. [3] So I want you to know that no one speaking by the Spirit of God will curse Jesus, and no one can say Jesus is Lord, except by the Holy Spirit.

[4] There are different kinds of spiritual gifts, but the same Spirit is the source of them all.[5] There are different kinds of service, but we serve the same Lord. [6] God works in different ways, but it is the same God who does the work in all of us.

[7] A spiritual gift is given to each of us so we can help each other. [8] To one person the Spirit gives the ability to give wise advice[b]; to another the same Spirit gives a message of special knowledge.[c] [9] The same Spirit gives great faith to another, and to someone else the one Spirit gives the gift of healing. [10] He gives one person the power to perform miracles, and another the ability to prophesy. He

gives someone else the ability to discern whether a message is from the Spirit of God or from another spirit. Still another person is given the ability to speak in unknown languages,[d] while another is given the ability to interpret what is being said. 11 It is the one and only Spirit who distributes all these gifts. He alone decides which gift each person should have.

12 The human body has many parts, but the many parts make up one whole body. So it is with the body of Christ. 13 Some of us are Jews, some are Gentiles,[e] some are slaves, and some are free. But we have all been baptized into one body by one Spirit, and we all share the same Spirit.[f]

14 Yes, the body has many different parts, not just one part. 15 If the foot says, "I am not a part of the body because I am not a hand," that does not make it any less a part of the body. 16 And if the ear says, "I am not part of the body because I am not an eye," would that make it any less a part of the body? 17 If the whole body were an eye, how would you hear? Or if your whole body were an ear, how would you smell anything?

18 But our bodies have many parts, and God has put each part just where he wants it. 19 How strange a body would be if it had only one part! 20 Yes, there are many parts, but only one body. 21 The eye can never say to the hand, "I don't need you." The head can't say to the feet, "I don't need you."

22 In fact, some parts of the body that seem weakest and least important are actually the most necessary. 23 And the parts we regard as less honorable are those we clothe

with the greatest care. So we carefully protect those parts that should not be seen, [24] while the more honorable parts do not require this special care. So God has put the body together such that extra honor and care are given to those parts that have less dignity. [25] This makes for harmony among the members, so that all the members care for each other. [26] If one part suffers, all the parts suffer with it, and if one part is honored, all the parts are glad.

[27] All of you together are Christ's body, and each of you is a part of it. [28] Here are some of the parts God has appointed for the church:
first are apostles,
second are prophets,
third are teachers,
then those who do miracles,
those who have the gift of healing,
those who can help others,
those who have the gift of leadership,
those who speak in unknown languages.
[29] Are we all apostles? Are we all prophets? Are we all teachers? Do we all have the power to do miracles? [30] Do we all have the gift of healing? Do we all have the ability to speak in unknown languages? Do we all have the ability to interpret unknown languages? Of course not! [31] So you should earnestly desire the most helpful gifts.
But now let me show you a way of life that is best of all.

CONCLUSION:

The fact of the matter is that not one ministry, not one human being, not one church, it does not matter if there are 1 billion members can claim to have all that it takes to reach the harvest field. We need to reach out within our local teams and outside our teams to carry out the assignment the Lord has graciously given unto us to accomplish.

Reach out today beyond your comfort zone in love.

Prayer: Dear Lord God, we pray today for your body of believers spread around the whole wide world. Lord, we speak to the spirit of competition that has invaded your body of believers, we resist this spirit and command it out by the authority in the name of Jesus Christ and we call forth the spirit of team work in unity of spirit and love beyond boundaries in Jesus name, amen

Shalom!

Monday Ogwuojo Ogbe – E-discipleship at Otakada.org

Chapter 9 - The gift of the Holy Spirit — Rejection of this awesome gift by any church in this era is an acceptance of Powerlessness, Frustration and Fruitlessness in our WORK and WALK with the Lord.

"True spiritual unity is based on unity of function, purpose, and love for one another, not just on agreement about every doctrine." – Rick Joyner

Introduction

We are dealing with division in body of Christ as a result of our understanding, working and application of the personality of the Holy Spirit, the third person of the trinity in our dispensation.

Key verses:

John 14:26 But the Helper, the Holy Spirit, whom the Father will send in My name, He will teach you all things, and bring to your remembrance all things that I said to you

John 15:26 – "But when the Helper comes, whom I shall send to you from the Father, the Spirit of truth who proceeds from the Father, He will testify of Me.

John 16:7 when Jesus said, "But I tell you the truth, it is to your advantage that I go away; for if I do not go away, the Helper (Prakletos) shall not come to you, but if I go, I will send Him to you." The Holy Spirit is a parakletos for Christians.

John 20:21-22 So Jesus said to them again, "Peace to you! As the Father has sent Me, I Also send you." And when He had said this, He breathed on them, and said to them, "Receive the Holy Spirit.

2 Corinthians 1:3-4: "Blessed be the God and Father of our Lord Jesus Christ, the Father of mercies and the God of all comfort; who comforts us in all our affliction so that we may be able to comfort those who are in any affliction with the comfort with which we ourselves are comforted by God."

Acts 1:4-5,8 – And being assembled together with them, He commanded them not to depart from Jerusalem, but wait for the Promise of the Father, " which," He said, "you have heard from Me; for John truly baptized with water, but you shall be baptized with the Holy Spirit not many days from now." But you shall receive power when the Holy Spirit has come upon you; and you shall be witnesses to Me in Jerusalem, and in all Judea and Samaria, and to the end of the earth."

Acts 2:1-4, 38-39 When the Day of Pentecost had fully come, they were all with one accord in one place. And suddenly there came a sound from heaven, as of a rushing mighty wind, and it filled the whole house where they were sitting. Then there appeared to them divided tongues as of fire, and one sat upon each of them. And they were all filled with the Holy Spirit and began to speak with other tongues, as the Spirit gave them utterance. 38 The Peter said to them, "Repent, and let everyone of you be baptized in the name of Jesus Christ for the remission of sins; and you shall receive the gift of the Holy Spirit. For the promise is to you and to your children, and to all who are afar off, as many as the Lord our God will call."

Acts 4: 31 And when they had prayed, the place where they were assembled together was shaken; and they were all filled with the Holy Spirit, and they spoke the word of God with boldness.

Acts 8:15 –20 Now when the apostles who were at Jerusalem heard that Samaria had received the word of God, they sent Peter and John to them, who, when the had come down, prayed for them that they might receive the Holy Spirit. For as yet He had fallen upon none of them. They had only been baptized in the name of the Lord Jesus. Then the laid hands on them, and they received the Holy Spirit. And when Simon saw that through the laying on of the apostles hands the Holy Spirit was given, he offered them money, saying, "Give me this power also, that anyone on whom I lay hands may receive the Holy Spirit." But Peter said to him, "Your money perish with you, because you thought that the gift of God could be purchased with money!

Acts 9: 17-18,31 And Ananias went his way and entered the house; and laying his hands on him he said, "Brother Saul, the Lord Jesus, who appeared to you on the road as you came, has sent me that you may receive your sight and be filled with the Holy Spirit." Immediately there fell from his eyes something like scales, and he received his sight at once; and he arose and was baptized.31 Then the churches throughout all Judea, Galilee, and Samaria had peace and were edified. And walking in the fear of the Lord and in the comfort of the Holy Spirit, they were multiplied.

Acts 10: 44-47 While Peter was still speaking these words, the Holy Spirit fell upon all those who heard the word. And those of the circumcision who believed were astonished, as many as came with Peter, because the gift of the Holy Spirit had been poured out on the Gentiles also. 46 For they heard them speak with tongues and magnify God. Then Peter answered, "Can anyone forbid water, that these should not be baptized who have received the Holy Spirit just as we have?"

Acts 13:2,3 As the ministered to the Lord and fasted, the Holy Spirit said, 'Now separate to Me Barnabas and Saul for the work to which I have called them." 3 Then, having fasted and prayed, and laid hands on them, they sent them away.

Acts 19:1-6 – And it happened, while Apollos was at Corinth, that Paul, having passed through the upper regions, came to Ephesus. And finding some disciples he said to them, "Did you receive the Holy Spirit when you believed?" So they said to him, "We have not so much as heard whether there is a Holy Spirit." And he said to them, "Into John's baptism." The Paul said, "John indeed baptized with a baptism of repentance, saying to the people that they should believe on Him who would come after him, that is, on Christ Jesus." When they heard this, they were baptized in the name of the Lord Jesus. And when Paul had laid hands on them, the Holy Spirit came upon them, and the spoke with tongues and prophesied.

We have brought this up at this stage because of the importance of the subject of the Holy Spirit. Nothing has divided bible believing Christians even within the same church setting like the subject of the Holy Spirit.

The devil has gotten us exactly where he wanted us- In the position of helplessness, hopelessness, powerlessness and defeat on all fronts. We have settled nicely and comfortably into running our Christian race on one cylinder with an engine that has capacity for 16 cylinders on full throttle.

We cannot even begin to contemplate what we loss by relegating the ministry of the Holy Spirit to the back seat in our everyday lives. Yet, it is a gift which we can decide to accept or reject, we will still make heaven. We will still struggle with ministry, pretending everything is ok, we will still continue to procrastinate on witnessing to the Lord in our sphere of influence, we will still be powerless as it relates to bringing comfort to those who are comfortless. We will continue to struggle with healing the sick and bringing light where there is darkness.

We will continue to preach without conviction that only the Holy Spirit can bring to the hearers. We will continue to preach and teach without real transformation in the lives of the listeners. We will continue to go on the field for evangelism without the supernatural accompanying the efforts. We will continue to be blunt to the promptings, leadings and speaking of the Holy Spirit on very personal issue we can't discuss with anyone. we will still continue to go along with the hustle and the hassle that everyone else faces as humans here on earth without divine electricity or powerhouse that can distinguish us from the dying and decaying world around. It's a choice between daylight and darkness. It is a choice between working and walking in blindness in broad day light.

Are we still surprised that we are taking casualties on all fronts because as the saying goes, my priest is permitted to perish for lack of knowledge the Lord God declares in the book of Hosea 4:6 because we have ignored the instructions in His word.

The world is crying and weeping for the manifestation of the sons of God.
Read – Romans 8:1-11, 22-25 The Message (MSG)

The Solution Is Life on God's Terms

8 [1-2] With the arrival of Jesus, the Messiah, that fateful dilemma is resolved. Those who enter into Christ's being-here-for-us no longer have to live under a continuous, low-lying black cloud. A new power is in operation. The Spirit of life in Christ, like a strong wind, has magnificently cleared the air, freeing you from a fated lifetime of brutal tyranny at the hands of sin and death.
[3-4] **God went for the jugular when he sent his own Son. He didn't deal with the problem as something remote and unimportant. In his Son, Jesus, he personally took on the human condition, entered the disordered mess of struggling humanity in order to set it right once and for all. The law code, weakened as it always was by fractured human nature, could never have done that.**

The law always ended up being used as a Band-Aid on sin instead of a deep healing of it. And now what the law code asked for but we couldn't deliver is accomplished as we, instead of redoubling our own efforts, simply embrace what the Spirit is doing in us.

5-8 Those who think they can do it on their own end up obsessed with measuring their own moral muscle but never get around to exercising it in real life. Those who trust God's action in them find that God's Spirit is in them—living and breathing God! Obsession with self in these matters is a dead end; attention to God leads us out into the open, into a spacious, free life. Focusing on the self is the opposite of focusing on God. **Anyone completely absorbed in self ignores God, ends up thinking more about self than God. That person ignores who God is and what he is doing. And God isn't pleased at being ignored.**

9-11 But if God himself has taken up residence in your life, you can hardly be thinking more of yourself than of him. Anyone, of course, who has not welcomed this invisible but clearly present God, the Spirit of Christ, won't know what we're talking about. But for you who welcome him, in whom he dwells—even though you still experience all the limitations of sin—you yourself experience life on God's terms. It stands to reason, doesn't it, that if the alive-and-present God who raised Jesus from the dead moves into your life, he'll do the same thing in you that he did in Jesus, bringing you alive to himself? When God lives and breathes in you (and he does, as surely as he did in Jesus), you are delivered from that dead life. With his Spirit living in you, your body will be as alive as Christ's!

22-25 All around us we observe a pregnant creation. The difficult times of pain throughout the world are simply birth pangs. **But it's not only around us; it's *within* us. The**

Spirit of God is arousing us within. We're also feeling the birth pangs. These sterile and barren bodies of ours are yearning for full deliverance. That is why waiting does not diminish us, any more than waiting diminishes a pregnant mother. We are enlarged in the waiting. We, of course, don't see what is enlarging us. But the longer we wait, the larger we become, and the more joyful our expectancy.

26-28 Meanwhile, the moment we get tired in the waiting, God's Spirit is right alongside helping us along. If we don't know how or what to pray, it doesn't matter. He does our praying in and for us, making prayer out of our wordless sighs, our aching groans. He knows us far better than we know ourselves, knows our pregnant condition, and keeps us present before God. That's why we can be so sure that every detail in our lives of love for God is worked into something good.

CONCLUSION:

The world seeks the supernatural but can't find it even in our churches and they will run to the counterfeit power from the realm of wickedness. We can't take the world for Christ without the continues outpouring, infilling, empowerment and leading of the Holy Spirit in our lives.

Mission work and going to make disciples begins with the Holy Spirit, is sustained by the Holy Spirit, is directed and accomplished by the Holy Spirit. There is no other way....

Brothers, and sisters, don't be satisfied with water baptism, kneel down today and ask for the baptism of the Holy Spirit. You need this for effectiveness in intercession, you need Him for service unto the Lord, you need his help when discouraged... this is the era of the Holy Spirit, the third person of the trinity.. Do this and see how you fly like the eagle today!

It is a gift, fully paid for, God promised it for everyone who calls for it. When Philip went on crusade to Samaria, the people accepted Jesus and where baptized with water in the name of Jesus Christ but hands had to be laid on them by the apostles for them to receive the gift of the Holy Spirit. You can receive Him in your room without the laying on of hands by faith.. do this today in faith! Some of us have grieved the Holy Spirit and we have silenced Him out of our lives. Repent, ask Him to return, He is more than willing and waiting to come back to you in fullness. As Christians, we all have the Spirit of God rekindled in us..But for the work of ministry, we need Him in fullness and it is not one time affair. Take time to pray, fast and ask for His fullness today! We are agreeing with you in prayer. There is no distance in the realm of the spirit.

Prayer

Dear Lord God, Thank you for today, the gift of access and the gift of the Holy Spirit through Your Son Jesus Christ. We stand in agreement today with our brothers and sisters who are desirous of the baptism of the Holy Spirit with the divine attribute of power, presence, comfort, helper, intercessor, healer, deliverer, godly living, obedience, witnessing and service.

Lord baptize them today as You have promised. Let there be a sign that you have done this because no one remains the same with the full embody of the trinity in us and through us. Thank you for we have accepted this gift today by faith in You and the promise to them whom You have called and they have believed in Jesus name. We bring before You teachers in Christian gatherings around the world who have been blinded by the evil one, Lord, open their eyes today so that they can amend their ways and receive this gift as they begin to operate in new dimensions in You in Jesus name we have prayed with thanksgiving amen.

Shalom!

Monday Ogwuojo Ogbe – E-discipleship at Otakada.org

Chapter 10 - You are a King and a Priest to our God, A Dominion of Kings and Priests – Every Believer Is – Your Acceptance or Rejection of this FACT will affect Your Kingdom Service Outcomes and How God Responds to You – Believers have only two options: to live like slaves or to live as kings and priests.

"When we lose our identity in Christ, we lose our authority, when we lose our authority, we lose our confidence, when we lose our confidence and self-worth, we begin to wish to become like others or to outdo others and that breeds disunity in the body of Christ – The key to unity is Knowing thyself and thy place in the body of Christ" – Monday Ogwuojo Ogbe

Introduction

We are dealing with division in body of Christ as a result of this subject of kings and priest, our roles, who we are, how God sees us and what we do with who we are.

Key verses:

Revelation 1:5-7 The Message (MSG)
His Eyes Pouring Fire-Blaze
[4-7] I, John, am writing this to the seven churches in Asia province: All the best to you from The God Who Is, The God Who Was, and The God About to Arrive, and from the Seven Spirits assembled before his throne, and from Jesus Christ—Loyal Witness, Firstborn from the dead, Ruler of all earthly kings.
Glory and strength to Christ, who loves us,
who blood-washed our sins from our lives,
Who made us a Kingdom, Priests for his Father,
forever—and yes, he's on his way!
Riding the clouds, he'll be seen by every eye,
those who mocked and killed him will see him,
People from all nations and all times
will tear their clothes in lament.
Oh, Yes.

Revelation 5:9-10 The Message (MSG)
[6-10] So I looked, and there, surrounded by Throne, Animals, and Elders, was a Lamb, slaughtered but standing tall. Seven horns he had, and seven eyes, the Seven Spirits of God sent into all the earth. He came to the One Seated on

the Throne and took the scroll from his right hand. The moment he took the scroll, the Four Animals and Twenty-four Elders fell down and worshiped the Lamb. Each had a harp and each had a bowl, a gold bowl filled with incense, the prayers of God's holy people. And they sang a new song:
Worthy! Take the scroll, open its seals.
Slain! Paying in blood, you bought men and women,
Bought them back from all over the earth,
Bought them back for God.
Then you made them a Kingdom, Priests for our God,
Priest-kings to rule over the earth.

Exodus 19:5-6 The Message (MSG)
3-6 As Moses went up to meet God, God called down to him from the mountain: "Speak to the House of Jacob, tell the People of Israel: 'You have seen what I did to Egypt and how I carried you on eagles' wings and brought you to me. If you will listen obediently to what I say and keep my covenant, out of all peoples you'll be my special treasure. The whole Earth is mine to choose from, but you're special: a kingdom of priests, a holy nation.'
"This is what I want you to tell the People of Israel."

Hebrews 9:13-15 The Message (MSG)
Pointing to the Realities of Heaven
11-15 But when the Messiah arrived, high priest of the superior things of this new covenant, he bypassed the old tent and its trappings in this created world and went straight into heaven's "tent"—the true Holy Place—once and for all. He also bypassed the sacrifices consisting of goat and calf blood, instead using his own blood as the price to set us free once and for all. If that animal blood

and the other rituals of purification were effective in cleaning up certain matters of our religion and behavior, think how much more the blood of Christ cleans up our whole lives, inside and out. Through the Spirit, Christ offered himself as an unblemished sacrifice, freeing us from all those dead-end efforts to make ourselves respectable, so that we can live all out for God.

1 Peter 2:5-8 The Message (MSG)
The Stone
[4-8] Welcome to the living Stone, the source of life. The workmen took one look and threw it out; God set it in the place of honor. Present yourselves as building stones for the construction of a sanctuary vibrant with life, in which you'll serve as holy priests offering Christ-approved lives up to God. The Scriptures provide precedent:
Look! I'm setting a stone in Zion,
a cornerstone in the place of honor.
Whoever trusts in this stone as a foundation
will never have cause to regret it.
To you who trust him, he's a Stone to be proud of, but to those who refuse to trust him,
The stone the workmen threw out
is now the chief foundation stone.
For the untrusting it's
. . . a stone to trip over,
a boulder blocking the way.
They trip and fall because they refuse to obey, just as predicted

Romans 12:1-2 The Message (MSG)

Place Your Life Before God

12 [1-2] So here's what I want you to do, God helping you: Take your everyday, ordinary life—your sleeping, eating, going-to-work, and walking-around life—and place it before God as an offering. Embracing what God does for you is the best thing you can do for him. Don't become so well-adjusted to your culture that you fit into it without even thinking. Instead, fix your attention on God. You'll be changed from the inside out. Readily recognize what he wants from you, and quickly respond to it. Unlike the culture around you, always dragging you down to its level of immaturity, God brings the best out of you, develops well-formed maturity in you.

Introduction continues

Working for and walking with God rises and falls with our BELIEVE in who God says we are and what we do with that information in the SPACE God has assigned us to. Because of the importance of this subject to you and I as new covenant believers in Christ, I will be running this series in two parts, to conclude next week, God willing. Please stay with me on this one.

As citizens of God's kingdom, we are not just residents of His realm – we are kings and priests under the authority of Christ, our King and High Priest. – Revelation 1:5; 5:9-10. Our twofold role describes or portray or delineate precisely our God – given dominion on earth.

It has always been God's intention to make His people capable of developing a close and intimate relationship with Him while carrying out their purpose as His chosen instruments to expand His kingdom on earth.

Let us discover how God wants us to fulfill the two ministries of king and priest in the here and now. We will begin by exploring the connection between covenant and kingdom – between our relationship with God and our manifestation of His presence and power on the earth

The Covenant – Kingdom Connection

The connection between God's covenants with His people and their role in His kingdom is a thread that can be seen in both the Old and New Testaments. God told the Israelites, ***Now therefore, if you will indeed obey My voice and keep My covenant, then you shall be a special treasure to Me above all people; for all the earth is Mine. And you shall be to Me a kingdom of priests and a holy nation. (Exodus 19:5-6)***

The nation of Israel under Moses was a forerunner of the church with its roles of king and priest. God told the Israelites they were to be a "kingdom of priest" as they blessed the world. His main goal when He redeemed them from slavery in Egypt and brought them to Mount Sinai was to make a covenant with them, present them to Himself, and establish an everlasting relationship with them. To fulfill God's purpose, they needed to meet two conditions:

- **Obey His voice,**

and

- **Keep His covenant**

These conditions still distinguish a true child of God today. The key for us is that, while the Israelites were never able to uphold their part of the covenant, Christ has enabled us to fulfill the new covenant with God. (See Hebrews 9:13-15)

Through His sacrifice on the cross and resurrection, we receive the Holy Spirit to live within us, so we can love God, obey Him, and serve Him. This will have dealt with extensively in our last blog 10 of 7 series.

The covenant with our heavenly Father that Jesus provided is similar to the earlier covenant of sacrifice that God made with Abraham, because that covenant was one that was fulfilled only by God, unilaterally, though it required Abraham's faith. See Genesis 15
Human beings could never hold up their end of a covenant with God in their own strength and effort.

The most important requirement in any covenant is the commitment of sacrifice.

In the New Testament, we read,

To Christ Jesus who loved us and washed us from our sins in His own blood, and has made us kings and priests to His God and Father…(Revelation 1:5-6)
God never develops a permanent, personal relationships with anyone unless it is through a covenant of commitment. 'Gather My saints together to Me, those

who have made a covenant with Me by sacrifice" – Psalm 50:5)

All parties involved in the covenant must observe the conditions of the promise and be loyal to it and to each other. The same is true in all areas of life. For example, we cannot develop healthy family or ministry relationships without a commitment between those involved. This is why God requires obedience to the covenant, which can be summarized in one word: **loyalty.**
We must keep in mind that it is only through Christ's atonement and grace that we are able to remain in right standing with God. 1 Thessalonians 5:23-24

Without a covenant of commitment, it is impossible to have a permanent, biblical relationship with God.

Picture our covenant with God like a cross: The vertical post indicates our relationship with Him, and the horizontal one our relationship with our fellow believers and other people. If the vertical relationship is broken, the horizontal relationship is affected, and vice versa. Thus, when our relationship with our neighbor is damaged, our relationship with God also suffers injury.. Matthew 5:22-24

When God liberated the Israelites from slavery, He presented them with a special threefold offer to make them a treasure, a kingdom of priests, and a holy nation. The parts of this offer are inseparable – one cannot exist without the others. However, over the years, Israel was interested in the covenant more for the Promised Land and blessings God offered than it was in God Himself.

Unfortunately, the same is true for much of the church today.

Moreover, we find it had to rid ourselves of a "slavery" mentality, just as the Israelites did. It is our destiny to live as kings and priests. Instead, many believers lie like slaves – to sickness, depression, fear, rejection, sin, alcohol, drugs, illicit sex, pornography, food, and so on. They are kings in theory but slaves in practice. We must renew our minds to understand our kinship and priesthood, and surrender to God through a covenant of commitment, in order to receive our full inheritance in Him and experience His kingdom life.

Do I want to live as a king and a priest under Christ, or do i want to live as a slave under the condemnation and accusation of the enemy?

Believers have only two options: to live like slaves or to live as kings and priests.

Christ redeemed us to make us a kingdom of kings and priests.

There is a world just waiting for us to go and demonstrate that our supreme King and High Priest, Jesus Christ, lives today and that we are kings and priests in God's kingdom. Many people realize that their material possessions are not ultimately satisfying, and they know that their lives aren't working.

They are waiting for us to show them practical solutions and to manifest the power and authority we have in Christ to rule over the works of the devil; to show that the gospel of the kingdom is not mere theology, theory, or words, but that God's power can save people, heal their afflictions, and deliver them from bondage

We are God's representatives, called to bring heaven to earth wherever we go and in the midst of any situation we might be experiencing.

Let us now explore our two main roles in the kingdom. We begin in this 8th series with the office of the priest, because we cannot be kings until we have understood our priestly calling and have entered into it. The two roles are always interconnected.

If we have not fulfilled our responsibilities as priests, we will not be able to exercise our functions as kings.

What is a Priest?

You...are being built up...a holy priesthood, to offer up spiritual sacrifices acceptable to God through Jesus Christ. 1Peter 2:5

Our culture's idea of the priesthood is that it is a special calling for only a chosen few. Most of us think of a priest as a man who wears a black robe and a white collar and who is beyond the reach of the common person. He is not allowed to marry and must dedicate his life totally to God's service, and this lifestyle sets him apart from the rest of the people.

Since this image of a priest is so ingrained in us through our traditions, it is difficult for many believers to envision themselves as priests.

The New Testament concept of a priest is someone who presents spiritual sacrifices to God.

The work of Jesus Christ is for everyone who believes in Him and who confesses Him as Lord and Savior of his life. The priesthood of all believers is included in this work. We are priests of the almighty God, able to offer spiritual sacrifices to Him, thanks to the work of His Son.

It is important to recognize that there are priests in the kingdom of darkness, also – witches, sorcerers, wizards, and so forth – who sacrifice animals (and sometimes humans) to gain power from Satan so they can dominate and control people and situations. Some people who are in position to rule over others seek such "priest" in order to gain power.

They lend themselves to these practices that offend God. As priest and kings in God's kingdom, we are engaged in a war against the evil spiritual entities that are behind these satanic priests and that strive to gain dominion over all earthly territories.

Under the law of Moses, the kingship was given to the tribe of Judah and the priesthood was bestowed on the tribe of Levi. In those days, the king of Israel was not allowed to offer sacrifices or burn incense on the altar of the temple.

In Jesus Christ, the kingship and priesthood were united once again. Jesus served as King and Priest on earth, and He was highly exalted by God the Father as King od kings and Lord of lords after His resurrection and ascension.

On this basis of His priesthood, Jesus offered bread and wine during the last Supper with His disciples as a symbol of His body, which would be presented to God as a living sacrifice. See Matthew 26:26-29 He offered prayers, intercession, and Himself (see Hebrews 5:7; 9:14) to His heavenly Father by means of the Holy Spirit, constituting Himself both as the Priest who ministered the sacrifice and the Sacrifice itself. After making atonement for us, He entered the Holy of Holies in heaven on our behalf and as our predecessor (Hebrews 6:19-20), so that we can now enter God's presence, also. As we are called to be like Him in the world, we are priests and kings who extend His realm on earth.

"Consider the Apostle and High Priest of our confession, Christ Jesus" Hebrew 3:1. In this verse, we see two of the Lord's titles: Apostle – one sent by God to carry out a specific mission; and High Priest – one who is the mediator between God and man. Jesus has been our High Priest for more than two thousand years – and He continues to be our High Priest today. He is high priest "forever" Hebrew 5:6. His work continues in force because no one can approach, communicate with, or bring offerings to God without the mediation of a High Priest. There, we depend totally on Christ Hebrews 7:24-25;8:6

The following are some specific responsibilities to which we are called as priests in God's kingdom:

- Present Our Bodies as Living Sacrifices to God – Romans 12:1
- Means we are living and our lives are sacrifices unto God, this sacrifice is our reasonable service, given of our free will and made possible by God. It is something we ourselves are able to give. The altar is our heart and the sacrifice is ourselves. We will no longer offer our selves to things that displease God which are carnal but we will live for eternal purposes in carrying out God's good and perfect will and this will help us to prove what is good and acceptable will of God. He will carry out His will on the earth in our lives.
- Offer Sacrifices of Praise and Worship Hebrew 13:15
- We praise regardless of our circumstances

- Do Good and Share with Others Hebrew 13:16
-Giving that comes from the heart and takes us out of our comfort zones is a sacrifice that is pleasing to God

- Present Physical Gifts and Offerings to God – Hebrews 5:1

- Offer Prayer and Intercession – Hebrew 7:25

CONCLUSION:

Christ's present ministry in heaven is to make intercession on our behalf. He offered prayers, intercession, and Himself on earth, and now he lives to mediate for us. Since we are the extension of His ministry on earth, we also should prioritize prayers and intercession on behalf of other people. There are countless plans and purposes of God that cannot be carried out until we birth them through prayer.

Therefore, we must align our prayers with Christ's prayers...Expansion of the kingdom, salvation of souls, manifestation of Gods children, amongst other things. What an honor and privilege to be part of this ministry. This is not time to leave the job for the privilege few, this is time for us all to roll up the sleeve and swing to action in the kingdom. We do not have the time to **relax** in the pews so let us get into action today. The Lord is waiting. Are you ready?

Prayer:

Dear Lord God, thank You for the privilege of callings in as priest and kings in your kingdom here on earth. We pray for a willing and obedient heart to this role as we receive grace from you to excel in the enforcement of kingdom mandate upon us all in Jesus name, amen

Shalom!

Monday Ogwuojo Ogbe – E-discipleship at Otakada.org

Chapter 11 - You Are A King And A Priest To Our God, A Dominion Of Kings And Priests – Every Believer Is – Your Acceptance Or Rejection Of This Fact Will Affect Your Kingdom Service Outcomes And How God Responds To You – Believers Have Only Two Options: To Live Like Slaves Or To Live As Kings And Priests.

Introduction

We are dealing with division in body of Christ as a result of this subject of kings and priest, our roles, who we are, how God sees us and what we do with who we are. We continue with our discuss last week and now looking at who a king is.

It will be impossible to understand the concept if we do not first understand what Christ died to give us. What He is, He passed on to us to be His ambassadors here on earth. The world will be celebrating His birthday in two days and we would like to give clarity to His role as a **Prophet, A Priest and A King** and then we will understand our place relative to His. **The King of Kings came to make us kings and priest to our God..**

Key verses:

Isaiah 7:13-14

[13] Then Isaiah said, "Family of David, listen very carefully! Is it not enough that you would test the patience of humans? Will you now test the patience of my God? [14] But the Lord will still show you this sign:

The young woman is pregnant
and will give birth to a son.
She will name him Immanuel.

Isaiah 9:6-7 Living Bible (TLB)

[6] For unto us a child is born; unto us a son is given; and the government shall be upon his shoulder. These will be his royal titles: **"Wonderful," "Counselor," "The Mighty God," "The Everlasting Father," "The Prince of Peace."** [7] **His ever-expanding, peaceful government will never end. He will rule with perfect fairness and justice from the throne of his father David. He will bring true justice and peace to all the nations of the world. This is going to happen because the Lord of heaven's armies has dedicated himself to do it!**

Luke 2:8-14 Easy-to-Read Version (ERV)
Some Shepherds Hear About Jesus

[8] That night, some shepherds were out in the fields near Bethlehem watching their sheep. [9] An angel of the Lord appeared to them, and the glory of the Lord was shining around them. The shepherds were very afraid. [10] The angel said to them, "Don't be afraid. I have some very good news for you—news that will make everyone happy. [11] Today your Savior was born in David's town. He is the Messiah, the Lord. [12] This is how you will know him: You will find a baby wrapped in pieces of cloth and lying in a feeding box."

[13] Then a huge army of angels from heaven joined the first angel, and they were all praising God, saying,

[14] "Praise God in heaven,

and on earth let there be peace to the people who please him."

Matthew 1:18-24

[18] These are the facts concerning the birth of Jesus Christ: His mother, Mary, was engaged to be married to Joseph. But while she was still a virgin she became pregnant by the Holy Spirit. [19] Then Joseph, her fiancé,[b] being a man of stern principle,* decided to break the engagement but to do it quietly, as he didn't want to publicly disgrace her. [20] As he lay awake[c] considering this, he fell into a dream, and saw an angel standing beside him. "Joseph, son of David," the angel said, "don't hesitate to take Mary as your wife! For the child within her has been conceived by the Holy Spirit. [21] And she will have a Son, and you shall name him Jesus (meaning 'Savior'), for he will save his people from their sins. [22] This will fulfill God's message through his prophets—

[23] 'Listen! The virgin shall conceive a child! She shall give birth to a Son, and he shall be called "Emmanuel" (meaning "God is with us").'"

[24] When Joseph awoke, he did as the angel commanded and brought Mary home to be his wife, [25] but she remained a virgin until her Son was born; and Joseph named him "Jesus."

Luke 4:16-22 Ease-to-read

[16] When he came to the village of Nazareth, his boyhood home, he went as usual to the synagogue on Saturday, and stood up to read the Scriptures. [17] **The book of Isaiah the**

prophet was handed to him, and he opened it to the place where it says:

18-19 "The Spirit of the Lord is upon me; he has appointed me to preach Good News to the poor; he has sent me to heal the brokenhearted and to announce that captives shall be released and the blind shall see, that the downtrodden shall be freed from their oppressors, and that God is ready to give blessings to all who come to him."[b]

20 He closed the book and handed it back to the attendant and sat down, while everyone in the synagogue gazed at him intently. 21 Then he added, "These Scriptures came true today!"

22 All who were there spoke well of him and were amazed by the beautiful words that fell from his lips. "How can this be?" they asked. "Isn't this Joseph's son?"

Mark 16:

15 And then he told them, "You are to go into all the world and preach the Good News to everyone, everywhere. 16 Those who believe and are baptized will be saved. But those who refuse to believe will be condemned.

17 "And those who believe shall use my authority to cast out demons, and they shall speak new languages.[c] **18 They will be able even to handle snakes with safety, and if they drink anything poisonous, it won't hurt them; and they will be able to place their hands on the sick and heal them."**

As believers, we are consecrated to God and anointed
by the Holy Spirit just like Jesus was anointing.

Our anointing was also a sign that we are joined to Christ and share in his threefold mission as prophet, priest, and king.

The Israelites anointed their priests and kings with oil. They spoke of their prophets as being anointed with the spirit. Jesus, known as the Christ, the anointed one, fills all three roles. According to Luke, at the outset of his public ministry, Jesus read from Isaiah and claimed that the words referred to him:
The Spirit of the Lord is upon me,
because he has anointed me
to bring glad tidings to the poor.
Luke 4:18

A Prophet

A **prophet** is a messenger sent by God, a person who speaks for God. He or she witnesses to God, calls people to conversion, and may also foretell the future. Prophets often are killed for their message.

Jesus fits this description. He is none other than the Word of God in the flesh. He called the world to turn from sin and return to the Father and was put to death for it. In Scripture Jesus is presented as a prophet. Crowds identified him as "Jesus the prophet" (Matthew 21:11). He spoke of himself as a prophet: "No prophet is accepted in his own native place" (Luke 4:24). He foretold his passion and resurrection.

A Priest

A **priest** is a mediator, or bridge, between God and human beings. He offers sacrifice to God on behalf of all. Once a year on the Day of Atonement the Jewish high priest went into the Holy of Holies in the Temple. There he offered sacrifice to God to make up for his sins and the sins of the people.

The writer of the Letter to the Hebrews compared Jesus to Melchizedek, a mysterious, superior priest in the Old Testament who blessed Abraham. Jesus is the greatest high priest. Because he is both divine and human, Jesus is the perfect mediator. He is not only the perfect priest, holy and sinless, but the perfect sacrifice. The sacrifice of Jesus need never be made again. Jesus "entered once for all into the sanctuary, not with the blood of goats and calves but with his own blood, thus obtaining eternal redemption" (Hebrews 9:12). Jesus continues his role as priest. "He is always able to save those who approach God through him, since he lives forever to make intercession for them" (Hebrews 7:25).

A King

A **king** is a person who has supreme authority over a territory. When the Jewish people were ruled by kings, they became a nation. They longed for a Messiah who would again make them great.
A King does the following

- Rule with the rod of authority – The rod is the emblem of the kings authority Psalm 110:1
- Rule through prayer (This is where the role of priest and king overlap. We cannot do without

prayer...impossible – It must be based on scripture, it must be in synch with God's mind, empowered by the Holy Spirit

Jesus is spoken of as a king in the Gospels. Gabriel announced to Mary that the Lord God would give her son the throne of David his father, and he would rule over the house of Jacob forever. Magi looked for a newborn king of the Jews. When Jesus last entered Jerusalem, crowds hailed him as a king. He was arrested for making himself king, and the soldiers mocked him as one. When Pilate asked if he were king of the Jews, Jesus replied, "You say so," and he clarified, "My kingdom does not belong to this world" (John 18:36). The charge written against Jesus was "Jesus the Nazarene, the King of the Jews." Jesus announced the kingdom of God. His mission was to have God reign in the hearts of all and to have peace and justice in the world. Jesus exercised his royal office by serving.

When He was returning, He gave us authority over the kingdom of darkness so that we can enforce our kingly authority over the kingdom of darkness and occupy the territory till He returns.

CONCLUSION:

All believers are kings over the kingdom of God, enforcing kingdom mandate here on earth. No king is effective without authority. In Matthew 28, [18] He told his disciples, "I have been given all authority in heaven and earth. [19] Therefore go and make disciples in all the nations,[b] baptizing them into the name of the Father and of the Son and of the Holy Spirit, [20] and then teach these new disciples to obey all the commands I have given you; and be sure of this—that I am with you always, even to the end of the world."[c]

The transfer of authority was total and absolute. If we fail to enforce it, it will not be His fault but ours. We can choose to be puppets or a king enforcing God's kingdom authority over the territory unlawfully occupied by the evil one. What would you do today? Would you enforce it through the authority in the name of Jesus or will you back down and have the wicked one have his way? Jesus has done His part, we are the foot soldiers. May He find us faithful today as we remember His glorious arrival over 2000 years ago and His eminent return glory.

Prayer

Our heavenly Father, thank You for the privilege of belonging to the family of Your redeemed children here on earth. Thank You for sending Your Son to die once for us all. Thank You for Jesus and His miraculous birth. Lord, we pray for many who are celebrating Your birthday this week that do not have a relationship with You, Lord we ask that You draw them to Yourself, remove the veil from their eyes so that they may see, perceive and receive You as the only true God and Jesus Christ whom you sent to be our Prophet, Our Priest and our King and by the finished work, made all of us who believe in You, priest and king, reconciling humanity to You. We pray for Your children, that we will be faithful to the heavenly mandate as we humble ourselves under Your mighty hands so You can do with us as occasion demands until the end In Jesus name we have prayed. Amen

If you accept the challenge of Mathew 28:18, and Mark 16:15-19, I invite you to pray the following prayer of commitment as priest and kings unto our God whole heartedly out loud with FAITH today:

Jesus Christ, You are Lord, the Son of God, and the only way to heaven. You died on the cross for my sins and were raised from the dead on the third day. You paid the wages of my sins and redeemed me with Your precious blood. I surrender to You once more, Lord, and I present my body to God as a living sacrifice. I place myself at Your disposal. Do with me as You wish. Send me wherever You want me to go. From this day forward, I am Yours. Thank You for accepting me! Anoint me with authority and power so I can fulfill my calling as one of **Your kings and priests** who rules to expand Your kingdom on earth, today! I take my rod of authority and begin to use it right now. Amen!

Shalom!

Monday Ogwuojo Ogbe – E-discipleship at Otakada.org

Chapter 12 - The Old Rugged, Blood Stained Cross Of Christ Places A Compelling Demand On All Believers To Carry The Cross Every Day, Every Time And Every Where

Introduction

The Old Rugged, Blood Stained Cross of Christ Places a COMPELLING Demand on ALL Believers to CARRY the Cross Every Day, Every Time and Every Where.

Christ is love, when we truly encounter and experience the love of Christ in our lives, we become love agents and it becomes easy to carry the cross of Jesus Christ as we serve in the SPACE the Lord has allotted to us.

Note that Christ experienced and the Cross applied in our lives daily will nail and bury the coffin of disunity amongst Christian brethren for good.

All the problems with Christians and all the problems in the churches can be solved only by Christ experienced and the cross applied. There were divisions among the Corinthians because those believers paid their attention to gifts, signs, knowledge, and wisdom, but they very much neglected Christ and the cross.

Therefore, there were many problems. The more gifts and knowledge we have, the more problems we have. All the divisions and denominations were produced out of gifted persons. In the past four or five hundred years, whenever there was a deeper, gifted person, a division or sect was often created, and the more gifted the person was, the greater the division was.

Key verses:

Luke 9:23 Easy-to-Read Version (ERV)
23 Jesus continued to say to all of them, "Any of you who want to be my follower must stop thinking about yourself and what you want. You must be willing to carry the cross that is given to you every day for following me.

Mark 8:34-38 The Message (MSG)
34-37 Calling the crowd to join his disciples, he said, "Anyone who intends to come with me has to let me lead. You're not in the driver's seat; I am. Don't run from suffering; embrace it. Follow me and I'll show you how. Self-help is no help at all. Self-sacrifice is the way, my way, to saving yourself, your true self. What good would it do to get everything you want and lose you, the real you? What could you ever trade your soul for?
38 "If any of you are embarrassed over me and the way I'm leading you when you get around your fickle and unfocused friends, know that you'll be an even greater embarrassment to the Son of Man when he arrives in all the splendor of God, his Father, with an army of the holy angels."

Mark 10:21 The Message (MSG)
21 Jesus looked him hard in the eye—and loved him! He said, "There's one thing left: Go sell whatever you own and give it to the poor. All your wealth will then be heavenly wealth. And come follow me."

1 Corinthians 1:17-21 The Message (MSG)

17 God didn't send me out to collect a following for myself, but to preach the Message of what he has done, collecting a following for him. And he didn't send me to do it with a lot of fancy rhetoric of my own, lest the powerful action at the center—Christ on the Cross—be trivialized into mere words.

18-21 The Message that points to Christ on the Cross seems like sheer silliness to those hell-bent on destruction, but for those on the way of salvation it makes perfect sense. This is the way God works, and most powerfully as it turns out. It's written,

I'll turn conventional wisdom on its head, I'll expose so-called experts as crackpots.

So where can you find someone truly wise, truly educated, truly intelligent in this day and age? Hasn't God exposed it all as pretentious nonsense? Since the world in all its fancy wisdom never had a clue when it came to knowing God, God in his wisdom took delight in using what the world considered dumb—preaching, of all things!—to bring those who trust him into the way of salvation.

Galatians 6:12-16 The Message (MSG)

11-13 Now, in these last sentences, I want to emphasize in the bold scrawls of my personal handwriting the immense importance of what I have written to you. These people who are attempting to force the ways of circumcision on you have only one motive: They want an easy way to look good before others, lacking the courage to live by a faith that shares Christ's suffering and death. All their talk about the law is gas. They themselves don't keep the law! And they are highly selective in the laws they do observe. They only want you to be circumcised so they can boast of their success in recruiting you to their side. That is contemptible!

14-16 For my part, I am going to boast about nothing but the Cross of our Master, Jesus Christ. Because of that Cross, I have been crucified in relation to the world, set free from the stifling atmosphere of pleasing others and fitting into the little patterns that they dictate. Can't you see the central issue in all this? It is not what you and I do—submit to circumcision, reject circumcision. It is what God is doing, and he is creating something totally new, a free life! All who walk by this standard are the true Israel of God—his chosen people. Peace and mercy on them!

Hebrews 12:1-3 message
Do you see what this means—all these pioneers who blazed the way, all these veterans cheering us on? It means we'd better get on with it. Strip down, start running—and never quit! No extra spiritual fat, no parasitic sins. Keep your eyes on Jesus, who both began and finished this race we're in. Study how he did it. Because he never lost sight of where he was headed—that exhilarating finish in and with God—he could put up with anything along the way: Cross, shame, whatever. And now he's there, in the place of honor, right alongside God. When you find yourselves flagging in your faith, go over that story again, item by item, that long litany of hostility he plowed through. That will shoot adrenaline into your souls!

1 Corinthians 13:13
So these three things continue: faith, hope, and love. And the greatest of these is love.

Continued..

All the gifts mentioned in 1 Corinthians are spiritual gifts, not natural gifts. We may think that spiritual gifts can do no harm. In actuality, the gifts themselves do no harm, but the persons who are gifted often do a great deal of harm by the gifts. From the time of the Reformation through the present day, there has rarely been a very gifted person who has not created a denomination, sect, or division. We cannot say absolutely that there has not been an exception, but it is rather difficult for us to point one out. Almost every famous gifted person in the past centuries created a division by his gifts.

Although the gifts themselves are good, it depends on how we handle them. We must realize that Christ is the centre, and all the gifts are for Christ.

CONCLUSION:

In concluding this series, we will like to state that Spiritual gifts should not be a license to come up with a new doctrine or rubbish the old. Spiritual gifts should unify us and not divide us. In our engagement with the brethren, we should take up our cross daily and pour out the love that only Christ in us can produce with grace. As we draw to the close of the year 2019, I have a question for you. Do you believe in the cross of Christ? The cross is stained with the blood of Christ. The cross indicate love; The cross indicates forgiveness; the cross indicates humility and the cross places a demand on you are me who believe in Jesus Christ. What does it demand? The cross demands that we proclaim it to the dark world around us. If we believe, we will take action no matter the cost. Are we willing to pay the price of taking up our cross daily? May the Lord grant all of us renewed grace and vigor.

Happy new year in advance. Expect to see the 10 series in e-book and paperback within 30 days.

Prayer:

Dear Lord God, I pray for an encounter with You the living and everlasting God afresh. I pray that this experience with You, will leave a lasting footprint upon our hearts and minds. Cause us to experience the unconditional love You have for us by sending Your Son – Jesus Christ to die the death we were not qualified to die. Cause us to exemplify this love by taking up our cross and following You daily as Your ambassadors here on earth. As many that do not know you and are reading this post, Lord draw them to Yourself this day and may they experience this love, peace and joy that can only be found in You through Your Son Jesus Christ we have prayed. Amen!
Shalom!
Monday Ogwuojo Ogbe – E-discipleship at Otakada.org

Chapter 13 - The Christian Church – The church of Jesus Christ – The gate of hell shall not prevail against it

Introduction

We shall be looking at how it all began, what happened in the course of history, what do we have now and how can we get equipped to move forward with the call to unity and also to make disciples of all nations. In the course of the year, we shall be looking at the various Christian groups, what are the core believes, how do we defer and how can we reconcile and work together?

We will be looking at other believes outside the Christian faith. We will get to know what they stand for and how we can reach those for Christ as well. Virtually, we shall be travelling to India where there are thousands of gods, we shall be traveling to China, middle east, far east, Africa and the Americas. We shall get acquainted with the Buddhists, the Islamic faith and many more.

When we are done, you will begin to see them through their faith and the love of Christ because Christ came to die for these ones too so that next time you meet one on the plane, on the street, in the marketplace, in the classroom or hostel, you will be engaging with first class information that the Holy Spirit will energize us to reach them for Him both online and offline.

Let us begin with the church of Jesus Christ beginning today and in the course of several weeks going forward.

Key verses:

Matthew 16:15-20 Living Bible (TLB)
[15] Then he asked them, "Who do you think I am?"
[16] Simon Peter answered, "The Christ, the Messiah, the Son of the living God."
[17] **"God has blessed you, Simon, son of Jonah," Jesus said, "for my Father in heaven has personally revealed this to you—this is not from any human source.** [18] **You are Peter, a stone; and upon this rock I will build my church; and all the powers of hell shall not prevail against it.** [19] **And I will give you the keys of the Kingdom of Heaven; whatever doors you lock on earth shall be locked in heaven; and whatever doors you open on earth shall be open in heaven!"**
[20] Then he warned the disciples against telling others that he was the Messiah.

Matthew 24:1-14 Living Bible (TLB)
24 As Jesus was leaving the Temple grounds, his disciples came along and wanted to take him on a tour of the various Temple buildings.
[2] But he told them, "All these buildings will be knocked down, with not one stone left on top of another!"
[3] "When will this happen?" the disciples asked him later, as he sat on the slopes of the Mount of Olives. "What events will signal your return and the end of the world?"[a]
[4] Jesus told them, "Don't let anyone fool you. [5] For many will come claiming to be the Messiah and will lead many astray. [6] When you hear of wars beginning, this does not

signal my return; these must come, but the end is not yet. ⁷ The nations and kingdoms of the earth will rise against each other, and there will be famines and earthquakes in many places. ⁸ But all this will be only the beginning of the horrors to come.

⁹ **"Then you will be tortured and killed and hated all over the world because you are mine, ¹⁰ and many of you shall fall back into sin and betray and hate each other. ¹¹ And many false prophets will appear and lead many astray. ¹² Sin will be rampant everywhere and will cool the love of many. ¹³ But those enduring to the end shall be saved.**

¹⁴ **"And the Good News about the Kingdom will be preached throughout the whole world, so that all nations will hear it, and then, finally, the end will come.**

The Christian Church - History

Christian Church is an ecclesiological term generally used by Protestants to refer to the whole group of people belonging to Christianity throughout the history of Christianity. In this understanding, "Christian Church" does not refer to a particular Christian denomination but to the body of all believers. Some Christian traditions, however, believe that the term "Christian Church" or "Church" applies only to a specific historic Christian body or institution (e.g., the Catholic Church, the Eastern Orthodox Church, the Oriental Orthodox Churches, or the Assyrian Church of the East). The Four Marks of the Church first expressed in the Nicene Creed are that the Church is:

- **One (a unified Body of Particular Churches in full communion of doctrines and faith with each other),**

- **Holy (a sanctified and deified Body),**
- **Catholic (Universal and containing the fullness of Truth in itself), and**
- **Apostolic (its hierarchy, doctrines, and faith can be traced back to the Apostles).**

Thus, the majority of Christians globally (particularly of the apostolic churches listed above, as well as some Anglo-Catholics) consider the Christian Church as a visible and institutional enlivened with supernatural grace, while Protestants generally understand the Church to be an invisible reality not identifiable with any specific earthly institution, denomination, Others equate the Church with particular groups that share certain essential elements of doctrine and practice, though divided on other points of doctrine and government (such as the branch theory as taught by some Anglicans).

Most English translations of the New Testament generally use the word "church" as a translation of the Ancient Greek: ἐκκλησία, translit. ecclesia, found in the original Greek texts, which generally meant an "assembly". This term appears in two verses of the Gospel of Matthew, 24 verses of the Acts of the Apostles, 58 verses of the Pauline epistles (including the earliest instances of its use in relation to a Christian body), two verses of the Letter to the Hebrews, one verse of the Epistle of James, three verses of the Third Epistle of John, and 19 verses of the Book of Revelation. In total, ἐκκλησία appears in the New Testament text 114 times, although not every instance is a technical reference to the church.

In the New Testament, the term ἐκκλησία is used for local communities as well as in a universal sense to mean all believers. Traditionally, only orthodox believers are considered part of the true church, but convictions of what is orthodox have long varied, as many churches (not only the ones officially using the term "Orthodox" in their names) consider themselves to be orthodox and other Christians to be heterodox.

The Christian Church originated in Roman Judea in the first century AD, founded on the teachings of Jesus of Nazareth, who first gathered disciples. Those disciples later became known as "Christians"; according to Scripture, Jesus commanded them to spread his teachings to all the world. For most Christians, the holiday of Pentecost (an event that occurred after Jesus' ascension to Heaven) represents the birthday of the Church, signified by the descent of the Holy Spirit on gathered disciples. Acts 2:10 The leadership of the Christian Church began with the apostles.

Springing out of Second Temple Judaism, from Christianity's earliest days, Christians accepted non-Jews (Gentiles) without requiring them to fully adopt Jewish customs (such as circumcision). The parallels in the Jewish faith are the Proselytes, Godfearers, and Noahide. The conflict with Jewish religious authorities quickly led to the expulsion of the Christians from the synagogues in Jerusalem

The Church gradually spread throughout the Roman Empire and beyond, gaining major establishments in cities such as Jerusalem, Antioch, and Edessa. It also became a widely persecuted religion. It was condemned by the Jewish authorities as a heresy. The Roman authorities persecuted it because, like Judaism, its monotheistic teachings were fundamentally foreign to the polytheistic traditions of the ancient world and a challenge to the imperial cult. The Church grew rapidly until finally legalized and then promoted by Emperors Constantine and Theodosius I in the 4th century as the state church of the Roman Empire.

Already in the 2nd century, Christians denounced teachings that they saw as heresies, especially Gnosticism but also Montanism. Ignatius of Antioch at the beginning of that century and Irenaeus at the end saw union with the bishops as the test of correct Christian faith. After legalization of the Church in the 4th century, the debate between Arianism and Trinitarianism, with the emperors favouring now one side now the other, was a major controversy.

Prayer:

Dear Lord God, too much water has gone under the bridge but we stand on the promise that the gates of hell shall not prevail against Your church. Thank You for keeping to this promise through the ages and what You have started, You will accomplish to the glory and honour of Your name, in Jesus name we have prayed. Amen

Shalom!

Monday Ogwuojo Ogbe – E-discipleship at Otakada.org

Chapter 14 - The Christian Church – First Schism – Difference Between Catholics And Protestants – Aim For Reconciled Diversity

Introduction

We are looking at the first breakup or schism that occurred and what led up to it. We will highlight eight (8) major differences that divide the Catholics and the protestants. Our prayer and aim is for the brethren to come to a state of reconciled diversity in our drive to carry out the mandate Jesus Christ died to give us all and has mandated us as His followers to go and do likewise.

Key verses:

Matthew 16:15-20 Living Bible (TLB)
15 Then he asked them, "Who do you think I am?"
16 Simon Peter answered, "The Christ, the Messiah, the Son of the living God."
17 "God has blessed you, Simon, son of Jonah," Jesus said, "for my Father in heaven has personally revealed this to you—this is not from any human source. 18 You are Peter, a stone; and upon this rock I will build my church; and all the powers of hell shall not prevail against it. 19 And I will give you the keys of the Kingdom of Heaven; whatever doors you lock on earth shall be locked in heaven; and whatever doors you open on earth shall be open in heaven!"

20 Then he warned the disciples against telling others that he was the Messiah.

Matthew 15:1-14 Living Bible(TLB)
1 Some Pharisees and other Jewish leaders now arrived from Jerusalem to interview Jesus.
2 "Why do your disciples disobey the ancient Jewish traditions?" they demanded. "For they ignore our ritual of ceremonial handwashing before they eat." 3 He replied, "And why do your traditions violate the direct commandments of God? 4 For instance, God's law is 'Honor your father and mother; anyone who reviles his parents must die.' 5-6 But you say, 'Even if your parents are in need, you may give their support money to the church[a] instead.' And so, by your man-made rule, you nullify the direct command of God to honor and care for your parents. 7 You hypocrites! Well did Isaiah prophesy of you, 8 'These people say they honor me, but their hearts are far away. 9 Their worship is worthless, for they teach their man-made laws instead of those from God."
10 Then Jesus called to the crowds and said, "Listen to what I say and try to understand: 11 You aren't made unholy by eating nonkosher food! It is what you *say* and *think* that makes you unclean."
12 Then the disciples came and told him, "You offended the Pharisees by that remark."
13-14 Jesus replied, "Every plant not planted by my Father shall be rooted up, so ignore them. They are blind guides leading the blind, and both will fall into a ditch."

The main differences between Catholics and Protestants

Both Catholics and Protestants worship the same God, but the principles of faith are different. Five hundred years after the Reformation, there are still painful divisions between Protestants and Catholics.

In Germany, the country of the Reformation, a deep animosity divided Catholic and Protestant Christians up until a few decades ago. This division had deepened over the centuries through religious conflicts and wars.

It all started when Reformation took place, 500 years ago, as Martin Luther (1483-1546) tried to reform the Catholic Church. His attempt to do so instead led to a schism in the church.

On October 31, 1517, the publication of his Ninety-Five Theses, which outlined different abusive practices of the church, is considered the founding event that led to this division in Germany and the creation of the Evangelical Church.

Here are the eight main differences:

1. Understanding of the Bible
Catholicism and Protestantism have distinct views on the meaning and the authority of the Bible. For Protestant Christians, Luther made clear that the Bible is the **"Sola Skriptura,"** God's only book, in which He provided His revelations to the people and which allows them to enter in communion with Him.

Catholics, on the other hand, do not base their beliefs on the Bible alone. Along with the Holy Scripture, they are additionally bound by the **traditions** of the Roman Catholic Church.

2. Understanding the church

Catholics and Protestants have a different view on the nature of the church. The word **"catholic"** means **"all-embracing,"** and the Catholic Church sees itself as the only true church worldwide, under the leadership of the pope. In contrast, the Protestant Churches which have emerged from Reformation, also called **"Evangelical,"** which means **"according to the Gospel,"** do not make up one united Church. There are rather several tens of thousands of different denominations around the world. Officially, all of these many churches are considered equal.

3. The pope

Protestants are not open at all to papal primacy. According to the Evangelical view, this dogma contradicts statements in the Bible.

Catholics see in the pope the successor of the Apostle Peter, the first head of their Church, who was appointed by Jesus. The papal office is justified by an allegedly unbroken chain of consecrations, ranging from the first century to the present.

4. Understanding of the office

This continuous chain, known as the apostolic succession, is overall significant for different spiritual offices in the Catholic Church. With the Sacrament of Holy Orders, bishops, priests and deacons receive a lifelong seal of God giving them sacramental authority over Catholic laypeople. This consecration can only be given to men.

Protestants do not consecrate specific persons into office, but rather accept the principle that priesthood can be transferred to every believer – even to women.

5. Eucharist or Lord's Supper

The Catholics' views on the spiritual office are reflected in the Eucharist, or Holy Communion, a rite commemorating the Last Supper of Jesus with his disciples before his crucifixion. Once consecrated by a priest in the name of Jesus, bread and wine become the body and blood of Christ. Non-Catholics may not participate in Communion. In the Protest Church, every baptized person is invited to share and is allowed to lead the Lord's Supper. This approach is not accepted by Catholics.

Additionally, Eucharist has a different meaning for Catholics and Protestants. The bread, known as the Host, embodies Jesus and can therefore be prayed to. For Protestants, the ritual only serves to commemorate Jesus' death and resurrection.

6. Sacraments

In the Roman Catholic Church, there are seven solemn rites, called sacraments: **baptism, confirmation, the Eucharist, matrimony, penance, holy orders and extreme unction.** The church believes these sacraments were instituted by Jesus and that they confer God's grace. Most Protestant churches only practice two of these sacraments: **baptism and the Eucharist (called Lord's Supper).** They are perceived as symbolic rituals through which God delivers the Gospel. They are accepted through faith.

7. Marian dogmas and the worship of Saints

The Roman Catholic Church reveres Mary, the mother of Jesus, as **"Queen of Heaven."** However, there are few biblical references to support the Catholic Marian dogmas – which include the Immaculate Conception, her perpetual virginity and her Assumption into heaven. This is why they are rejected by Protestants.

The Catholic Church also practices the veneration of saints. Dead models of faith, recognized as **"saint"** by the church through canonization, can be prayed to for help in maintaining faith in God. There are over 4,000 saints. Their remains are considered holy relics which are venerated. This veneration is also categorically by the Protestant Church as unbiblical. According to Reformation views, every person may and should pray directly to God.

8. Celibacy

All main world religions integrate in some way the concept of celibacy, the vow of abstaining from marriage and sexual relations, and the Catholic and Protestant churches are no exception. In the Catholic Church, celibacy is obligatory for priests. It is seen as a symbol of the undivided succession of Christ.

The Protestant Church rejects this obligation for priests. Martin Luther already demanded its abolition as early as 1520. He made a decisive personal contribution to this end in 1525: The former monk married the former nun Katharina von Bora. Initially unsure of whether he should marry, Luther finally determined that "his marriage would please his father, rile the pope, cause the angels to laugh, and the devils to weep."

Conclusion

I will refer the readers to take a critical look at Matthew 15:1-14 and several other scriptures including Galatians 1:14. Our coordinates as Gods children should be drawn from the Holy Scriptures and not by human tradition. May the Lord grant wisdom and the grace for us all to see ourselves as one before God and Jesus Christ whom He sent to deliver mankind. Everything else should be secondary to this sole objective and understanding.

Prayer

Dear Lord God, we present Your body of believers around the world before You today, Lord, speak to us all in ascents loud and clear, help us to let go of institution, tradition and vein imagination and help us to focus on You the author and finisher of our faith and Jesus Christ whom You sent to deliver mankind. We tear down these invisible and man-made walls that divide us. Help us to be reconciled to You and to one another despite our diversity in Jesus name I have prayed (Amen)

Shalom!

Chapter 15 - Who Are The True Worshipers, Where Can We Find Them?

Introduction

Who are the true worshipers of God and where can they be found? The best answer comes from the book of John 4:23-25... lets dive in

Key Verse

John 4:23-25

But the time is coming—it has, in fact, come—when what you're called will not matter and where you go to worship will not matter. "It's who you are and the way you live that count before God. Your worship must engage your spirit in the pursuit of truth. That's the kind of people the Father is out looking for: those who are simply and honestly themselves before him in their worship. God is sheer being itself—Spirit. Those who worship him must do it out of their very being, their spirits, their true selves, in adoration."

Full text

John 4: 16-26

16 He said, "Go call your husband and then come back."
17-18 "I have no husband," she said.
"That's nicely put: 'I have no husband.' You've had five husbands, and the man you're living with now isn't even your husband. You spoke the truth there, sure enough."
19-20 "Oh, so you're a prophet! Well, tell me this: Our ancestors worshiped God at this mountain, but you Jews insist that Jerusalem is the only place for worship, right?"

21-23 "Believe me, woman, the time is coming when you Samaritans will worship the Father neither here at this mountain nor there in Jerusalem. You worship guessing in the dark; we Jews worship in the clear light of day. God's way of salvation is made available through the Jews. But the time is coming—it has, in fact, come—when what you're called will not matter and where you go to worship will not matter.

23-24 "It's who you are and the way you live that count before God. Your worship must engage your spirit in the pursuit of truth. That's the kind of people the Father is out looking for: those who are simply and honestly themselves before him in their worship. God is sheer being itself—Spirit. Those who worship him must do it out of their very being, their spirits, their true selves, in adoration."

25 The woman said, "I don't know about that. I do know that the Messiah is coming. When he arrives, we'll get the whole story."

26 "I am he," said Jesus. "You don't have to wait any longer or look any further."

John 6:41-71

41 The Jews then complained about Him, because He said, "I am the bread which came down from heaven."

42 And they said, "Is not this Jesus, the son of Joseph, whose father and mother we know? How is it then that He says, 'I have come down from heaven'?"

43 Jesus therefore answered and said to them, "Do not murmur among yourselves.

44 No one can come to Me unless the Father who sent Me draws him; and I will raise him up at the last day.

45 It is written in the prophets, 'And they shall all be taught by God.' Therefore everyone who has heard and learned from the Father comes to Me.

46 Not that anyone has seen the Father, except He who is from God; He has seen the Father.

47 Most assuredly, I say to you, he who believes in Me has everlasting life.

48 I am the bread of life.

49 Your fathers ate the manna in the wilderness, and are dead.

50 This is the bread which comes down from heaven, that one may eat of it and not die.

51 I am the living bread which came down from heaven. If anyone eats of this bread, he will live forever; and the bread that I shall give is My flesh, which I shall give for the life of the world."

52 The Jews therefore quarreled among themselves, saying, "How can this Man give us His flesh to eat?"

53 Then Jesus said to them, "Most assuredly, I say to you, unless you eat the flesh of the Son of Man and drink His blood, you have no life in you.

54 Whoever eats My flesh and drinks My blood has eternal life, and I will raise him up at the last day.

55 For My flesh is food indeed, and My blood is drink indeed.

56 He who eats My flesh and drinks My blood abides in Me, and I in him.

57 As the living Father sent Me, and I live because of the Father, so he who feeds on Me will live because of Me.

58 This is the bread which came down from heaven—not as your fathers ate the manna, and are dead. He who eats this bread will live forever."

59 These things He said in the synagogue as He taught in Capernaum.

60 Therefore many of His disciples, when they heard this, said, "This is a hard saying; who can understand it?"

61 When Jesus knew in Himself that His disciples complained about this, He said to them, "Does this offend you?

62 What then if you should see the Son of Man ascend where He was before?

63 It is the Spirit who gives life; the flesh profits nothing. The words that I speak to you are spirit, and they are life.

64 But there are some of you who do not believe." For Jesus knew from the beginning who they were who did not believe, and who would betray Him.

65 And He said, "Therefore I have said to you that no one can come to Me unless it has been granted to him by My Father."

66 From that time many of His disciples went back and walked with Him no more.

67 Then Jesus said to the twelve, "Do you also want to go away?"

68 But Simon Peter answered Him, "Lord, to whom shall we go? You have the words of eternal life.

69 Also we have come to believe and know that You are the Christ, the Son of the living God."

70 Jesus answered them, "Did I not choose you, the twelve, and one of you is a devil?"

71 He spoke of Judas Iscariot, the son of Simon, for it was he who would betray Him, being one of the twelve.

Conclusion and prayer – The bible reference is self-explanatory. Now is the time to worship in spirit and in truth from wherever we are in the depth of our hearts Amen.
Shalom!

Chapter 16 - The Christian Church – Are Jehovah Witnesses Christians? Should We Open Channels of Engagement With Them?

Introduction

We are looking at the Jehovah Witnesses. What are their believes? Are they Christ Followers or not? Are their areas of mutual believe? Do we need to open windows or channels of engagement with the JWs? Let see...

Key verses

Deuteronomy 6:4 The Message (MSG)
⁴ Attention, Israel!
God, our God! God the one and only!

Exodus 3:14 The Message (MSG)
¹⁴ God said to Moses, **"I-AM-WHO-I-AM**. Tell the People of Israel, 'I-AM sent me to you.'"

John 8:58 The Message (MSG)
⁵⁸ "Believe me," said Jesus, **"I am who I am** long before Abraham was anything."

John 14:1-21 Living Bible (TLB)
"Let not your heart be troubled. You are trusting God, now trust in me. ²⁻³ There are many homes up there where my Father lives, and I am going to prepare them for your coming. When everything is ready, then I will come and

get you, so that you can always be with me where I am. If this weren't so, I would tell you plainly. ⁴ And you know where I am going and how to get there."

⁵ "No, we don't," Thomas said. "We haven't any idea where you are going, so how can we know the way?"

⁶ Jesus told him, "I am the Way—yes, and the Truth and the Life. No one can get to the Father except by means of me. ⁷ If you had known who I am, then you would have known who my Father is. From now on you know him—and have seen him!"

⁸ Philip said, "Sir, show us the Father and we will be satisfied."

⁹ Jesus replied, "Don't you even yet know who I am, Philip, even after all this time I have been with you? Anyone who has seen me has seen the Father! So why are you asking to see him? ¹⁰ Don't you believe that I am in the Father and the Father is in me? The words I say are not my own but are from my Father who lives in me. And he does his work through me. ¹¹ Just believe it—that I am in the Father and the Father is in me. Or else believe it because of the mighty miracles you have seen me do.

¹²⁻¹³ "In solemn truth I tell you, anyone believing in me shall do the same miracles I have done, and even greater ones, because I am going to be with the Father. You can ask him for *anything,* using my name, and I will do it, for this will bring praise to the Father because of what I, the Son, will do for you. ¹⁴ Yes, ask *anything,* using my name, and I will do it!

¹⁵⁻¹⁶ "If you love me, obey me; and I will ask the Father and he will give you another Comforter, and he will never leave you. ¹⁷ He is the Holy Spirit, the Spirit who leads into all truth. The world at large cannot receive him, for it isn't looking for him and doesn't recognize him. But you do, for

he lives with you now and some day shall be in you. [18] No, I will not abandon you or leave you as orphans in the storm—I will come to you. [19] In just a little while I will be gone from the world, but I will still be present with you. For I will live again—and you will too. [20] When I come back to life again, you will know that I am in my Father, and you in me, and I in you. [21] The one who obeys me is the one who loves me; and because he loves me, my Father will love him; and I will too, and I will reveal myself to him."

Matthew 16:15-20 Living Bible (TLB)
[15] Then he asked them, "Who do you think I am?"
[16] Simon Peter answered, "The Christ, the Messiah, the Son of the living God."
[17] **"God has blessed you, Simon, son of Jonah," Jesus said, "for my Father in heaven has personally revealed this to you—this is not from any human source. [18] You are Peter, a stone; and upon this rock I will build my church; and all the powers of hell shall not prevail against it. [19] And I will give you the keys of the Kingdom of Heaven; whatever doors you lock on earth shall be locked in heaven; and whatever doors you open on earth shall be open in heaven!"**
[20] Then he warned the disciples against telling others that he was the Messiah.

Acts 5:3-4 The Message (MSG)
[3-4] Peter said, "Ananias, how did Satan get you to **lie to the Holy Spirit** and secretly keep back part of the price of the field? Before you sold it, it was all yours, and after you sold it, the money was yours to do with as you wished. So what got into you to pull a trick like this? You didn't **lie to men but to God.**"

James 2:19-20 Living Bible (TLB)

[19] Are there still some among you who hold that "only believing" is enough? Believing in one God? Well, remember that the demons believe this too—so strongly that they tremble in terror! [20] Fool! When will you ever learn that "believing" is useless without *doing* what God wants you to? Faith that does not result in good deeds is not real faith.

Matthew 28:19 Living Bible (TLB)

[19] Therefore go and make disciples in all the nations,[a] baptizing them into the name of the **Father and of the Son and of the Holy Spirit,**

Inputs received from Jehovah Witness

These inputs are from Jehovah Witness website http://www.jw.org

As Jehovah's Witnesses, we strive to adhere to the form of Christianity that Jesus taught and that his apostles practiced. This article summarizes our basic beliefs.

- **We worship the one true and Almighty God, the Creator, whose** name is Jehovah. **(**Psalm 83:18; Revelation 4: 11**) He is the God of Abraham, Moses, and Jesus.** —Exodus 3:6; 32:11; John 20:17.

- **We recognize** the Bible as God's inspired message **to humans. (**John 17:17; 2 Timothy 3: 16**)**

We base our beliefs on all 66 of its books, which include both the "Old Testament" and the "New Testament." Professor Jason D. BeDuhn aptly described it when he wrote that Jehovah's Witnesses built "their system of belief and practice from the raw material of the Bible without predetermining what was to be found there." * While we accept the entire Bible, we are not fundamentalists. We recognize that parts of the Bible are written in figurative or symbolic language and are not to be understood literally. — Revelation 1:1.

- We follow the teachings and example of Jesus Christ and honor him as our Savior and as the Son of God. (Matthew 20:28; Acts 5: 31) Thus, we are Christians. (Acts 11:26) However, we have learned from the Bible that Jesus is not Almighty God and that there is no Scriptural basis for the Trinity doctrine. —John 14:28.

- The Kingdom of God. This is a real government in heaven, not a condition in the hearts of Christians. It will replace human governments and accomplish God's purpose for the earth. (Daniel 2: 44; Matthew 6: 9, 10) It will take these actions soon, for Bible prophecy indicates that we are living in "the last days." —2 Timothy 3: 1-5; Matthew 24: 3- 14. Jesus is the King of God's Kingdom in heaven. He began ruling in 1914. — Revelation 11:15.

- Deliverance from sin and death is possible through the ransom sacrifice of Jesus. (Matthew 20:28; Acts 4: 12) To benefit from that sacrifice, people must not only exercise faith in Jesus but also change their course of life and get baptized.

155

(Matthew 28:19, 20; John 3: 16; Acts 3: 19, 20) A person's works prove that his faith is alive. (James 2: 24,26) However, salvation cannot be earned — it comes through "the undeserved kindness of God." —Galatians 2: 16, 21.

- Jehovah God, Jesus Christ, and the faithful angels reside in the spirit realm. * (Psalm 103:19-21; Acts 7: 55) A relatively small number of people —144,000 —will be resurrected to life in heaven to rule with Jesus in the Kingdom. —Daniel 7: 27; 2 Timothy 2: 12; Revelation 5: 9, 10; 14: 1,3.   Earth. God created the earth to be mankind's eternal home. (Psalm 104:5; 115:16; Ecclesiastes 1:4) God will bless obedient people with perfect health and everlasting life in an earthly paradise. —Psalm 37:11, 34.

- Evil and suffering. These began when one of God's angels rebelled. (John 8: 44) This angel, who after his rebellion was called "Satan" and "Devil," persuaded the first human couple to join him, and the consequences have been disastrous for their descendants. (Genesis 3: 1-6; Romans 5: 12) In order to settle the moral issues raised by Satan, God has allowed evil and suffering, but He will not permit them to continue forever.

- People who die pass out of existence. (Psalm 146:4; Ecclesiastes 9: 5, 10) They do not suffer in a fiery hell of torment. God will bring billions back from death by means of a resurrection. (Acts 24:15) However, those who refuse to learn God's ways after being raised to life will be destroyed forever with no hope of a resurrection. — Revelation 20:14, 15.   Family. We adhere to

God's original standard of marriage as the union of one man and one woman, with sexual immorality being the only valid basis for divorce. (Matthew 19: 4-9) We are convinced that the wisdom found in the Bible helps families to succeed. —Ephesians 5:22– 6:1.

- Our worship. We do not venerate the cross or any other images. (Deuteronomy 4: 15- 19; 1 John 5: 21) Key aspects of our worship include the following:
  - Praying to God. —Philippians 4:6.
  - Reading and studying the Bible. —Psalm 1: 1-3.
  - Meditating on what we learn from the Bible. —Psalm 77:12.
  - Meeting together to pray, study the Bible, sing, express our faith, and encourage fellow Witnesses and others. —Colossians 3: 16; Hebrews 10:23- 25.
  - Preaching the "good news of the Kingdom." —Matthew 24:14.
  - Helping those in need. —James 2: 14- 17.
  - Constructing and maintaining Kingdom Halls and other facilities used to further our worldwide Bible educational work. — Psalm 127:1.
  - Sharing in disaster relief. —Acts 11:27- 30.
- Our organization. We are organized into congregations, each of which is overseen by a body of elders. However, the elders do not form a clergy class, and they are unsalaried. (Matthew 10:8; 23:8) We do not practice tithing, and no collections are ever taken at our meetings. (2 Corinthians 9:7) All our activities are supported

by anonymous donations. The Governing Body, a small group of mature Christians who serve at our world headquarters, provides direction for Jehovah's Witnesses worldwide. —Matthew 24:45.

- Our unity. We are globally united in our beliefs. (1 Corinthians 1: 10) We also work hard to have no social, ethnic, racial, or class divisions. (Acts 10:34, 35; James 2:4) Our unity allows for personal choice, though. Each Witness makes decisions in harmony with his or her own Bible-trained conscience. —Romans 14: 1-4; Hebrews 5: 14.

- Our conduct. We strive to show unselfish love in all our actions. (John 13:34, 35) We avoid practices that displease God, including the misuse of blood by taking blood transfusions. (Acts 15:28, 29; Galatians 5: 19- 21) We are peaceful and do not participate in warfare. (Matthew 5:9; Isaiah 2:4) We respect the government where we live and obey its laws as long as these do not call on us to disobey God's laws. —Matthew 22:21; Acts 5: 29.

- Our relationships with others. Jesus commanded: "You must love your neighbor as yourself." He also said that Christians "are no part of the world." (Matthew 22:39; John 17:16) So we try to "work what is good toward all," yet we remain strictly neutral in political affairs and avoid affiliation with other religions. (Galatians 6: 10; 2 Corinthians 6: 14) However, we respect the choices that others make in such matters. — Romans 14:12.

If you have further questions about the beliefs of Jehovah's Witnesses, you can read more about us on our website, contact one of our offices, **attend a** meeting at a Kingdom Hall near you, **or speak to one of the Witnesses in your area.**

Conclusion

What I can conclude from reading the JW doctrine are that they believe in God, They believe in Jesus as the Son of God and Jesus Christ is their savior hence they are Christians. Every other deviation is a matter of maturity, revelation and understanding. They do not believe in the trinity. Will that make a them a non-Christian? I don't think so. We all know the Holy Spirit is alive and well and working in our time and age. Even Jesus Disciples had difficulty understanding the concept of trinity as we read in John 14. Will I extend a hand of fellowship to the JW? Why not?

Will Jesus reject them because they do not believe in the trinity or if their understanding of the kingdom is screwed? Not the Jesus that I know.

Prayer

Dear Lord God, we present Your body of believers around the world before You today, Lord, help us to let go of petty differences but to focus on the high calling of God for our lives. Help us to accommodate those who have differing revelation from ours but rather seek points of agreement that does not compromise Jesus stand. Help us to be reconciled to You and to one another despite our diversity in Jesus name I have prayed (Amen)

Shalom!

Chapter 17 The Christian Church – Account of My Meeting with Prophet T.B Joshua of The Synagogue, Church Of All Nations (SCOAN)

Introduction

Prophet T.B Joshua

We are looking at The Synagogue, Church of all Nations pastored by **Prophet T.B Joshua**. What are their believes? Are they Christ Followers or not? Are their areas of mutual believe? Do we need to open windows or channels of engagement with SCOAN? Before I move on to the statement of faith, I will give account of my engagement with Prophet T.B Joshua in his office on Thursday, 15thof April 2010 at about 4 PM. Let us explore scripture first..

Key verses

MATTHEW 7:15-23 AMPLIFIED BIBLE (AMP)

A Tree and Its Fruit

¹⁵ "Beware of the false prophets, [teachers] who come to you dressed as sheep [appearing gentle and innocent], but inwardly are ravenous wolves. ¹⁶ By their fruit you will recognize them[that is, by their contrived doctrine and self-focus]. Do people pick grapes from thorn bushes or figs from thistles? ¹⁷ Even so, every healthy tree bears good fruit, but the unhealthy tree bears bad fruit. ¹⁸ A good tree cannot bear bad fruit, nor can a bad tree bear good fruit. ¹⁹ Every tree that does not bear good fruit is cut

down and thrown into the fire. [20] Therefore, by their fruit you will recognize them [as false prophets].

[21] "Not everyone who says to Me, 'Lord, Lord,' will enter the kingdom of heaven, but only he who does the will of My Father who is in heaven. [22] Many will say to Me on that day [when I judge them], 'Lord, Lord, have we not prophesied in Your name, and driven out demons in Your name, and done many miracles in Your name?' [23] And then I will declare to them publicly, 'I never knew you; depart from Me [you are banished from My presence], you who act wickedly[disregarding My commands].'

GALATIANS 5:16-26 AMPLIFIED BIBLE (AMP)

[16] But I say, walk *habitually* in the [Holy] Spirit [seek Him and be responsive to His guidance], and then you will certainly not carry out the desire of the [a]sinful nature [which responds impulsively without regard for God and His precepts]. [17] For the sinful nature has its desire which is opposed to the Spirit, and the [desire of the] Spirit opposes the [b]sinful nature; for these [two, the sinful nature and the Spirit] are in direct opposition to each other [continually in conflict], so that you [as believers] do not [always] do whatever [good things] you want to do. [18] But if you are guided *and* led by the Spirit, you are not subject to the Law. [19] Now the practices of the [c]sinful nature are *clearly* evident: they are sexual immorality, impurity, sensuality (total irresponsibility, lack of self-control), [20] [d]idolatry, [e]sorcery, hostility, strife, jealousy, fits of anger, disputes, dissensions, factions [that promote heresies], [21] envy, drunkenness, riotous behavior, and *other* things like these. I warn you beforehand, just as I did previously, that those who practice such things will not inherit the kingdom of God. [22] But the fruit of the Spirit [the result of His presence within us] is love [unselfish

concern for others], joy, [inner] peace, patience [not the ability to wait, but how we act while waiting], kindness, goodness, faithfulness, ²³ gentleness, self-control. Against such things there is no law. ²⁴ And those who belong to Christ Jesus have crucified the [f]sinful nature together with its passions and appetites.

²⁵ If we [claim to] live by the [Holy] Spirit, we must also walk by the Spirit [with personal integrity, godly character, and moral courage—our conduct empowered by the Holy Spirit]. ²⁶ We must not become conceited,
challenging or provoking one another, envying one another.

MARK 9:38-41 AMPLIFIED BIBLE (AMP)
DIRE WARNINGS

³⁸ John said to Him, "Teacher, we saw someone casting out demons in Your name, and we tried to stop him because he was not accompanying us [as Your disciple]." ³⁹ But Jesus said, "Do not stop him; for there is no one who will perform a miracle in My name, and be able soon afterward to speak evil of Me. ⁴⁰ For he who is not against us is for us. ⁴¹ For whoever gives you a cup of water to drink because of your name as followers of Christ, I assure you and most solemnly say to you, he will not lose his reward.

Genesis 1:26
Then God said, "**Let us make** a **man**—someone like ourselves,* to be the master of all life upon the earth and in the skies and in the seas."

John 17:1- Living Bible (TLB)
17 When Jesus had finished saying all these things he looked up to heaven and said, "Father, the time has come.

Reveal the glory of your Son so that he can give the glory back to you. [2] For you have given him authority over every man and woman in all the earth. He gives eternal life to each one you have given him. [3] And this is the way to have eternal life—by knowing you, the only true God, and Jesus Christ, the one you sent to earth! [4] I brought glory to you here on earth by doing everything you told me to. [5] And now, Father, reveal my glory as I stand in your presence, the glory we shared before the world began.

[6] "I have told these men all about you. They were in the world, but then you gave them to me. Actually, they were always yours, and you gave them to me; and they have obeyed you. [7] Now they know that everything I have is a gift from you, [8] for I have passed on to them the commands you gave me; and they accepted them and know of a certainty that I came down to earth from you, and they believe you sent me.

[9] "My plea is not for the world but for those you have given me because they belong to you. [10] And all of them, since they are mine, belong to you; and you have given them back to me with everything else of yours, and so *they are my glory!* [11] Now I am leaving the world, and leaving them behind, and coming to you. Holy Father, keep them in your own care—all those you have given me—so that they will be united just as we are, with none missing. [12] During my time here I have kept safe within your family all of these you gave me.[a] I guarded them so that not one perished, except the son of hell, as the Scriptures foretold.

[13] "And now I am coming to you. I have told them many things while I was with them so that they would be filled with my joy. [14] I have given them your commands. And the world hates them because they don't fit in with it, just as I don't. [15] I'm not asking you to take them out of the world,

but to keep them safe from Satan's power. [16] They are not part of this world any more than I am. [17] Make them pure and holy through teaching them your words of truth. [18] As you sent me into the world, I am sending them into the world, [19] and I consecrate myself to meet their need for growth in truth and holiness.

[20] "I am not praying for these alone but also for the future believers who will come to me because of the testimony of these. [21] My prayer for all of them is that they will be of one heart and mind, just as you and I are, Father—that just as you are in me and I am in you, so they will be in us, and the world will believe you sent me.

What was my mission to SCOAN?

Three months prior, the Lord had shown me 3 different revelations of the calamity that was to befall the Nigerian nation. He had instructed that intercession be made by selected churches in Nigeria. Seven churches were to be visited in each of the 36 states capital, including FCT, Abuja making 37. Twelve copies of the prayer book were handed to them for intercessors to intercede for revival in the land beginning with the church over a 36 months' period, which expired in 2012. The trip took me all around the country to 260 churches, 3120 copies of the prayer book were distributed. The mission took 12 days, 7000 km. SCOAN was the final church visited in Lagos. I was not able to see the prophet on the 14th and was rescheduled for the next day.

I was escorted to his office. There was no long wait, no red tapes, I did not see any body guard and his office was as humble as humble can be. I stated my mission, handed him the copies and he prayed that the lord will give me the voice to push the message through.

After that visit, I have worshiped on three occasion. His messages were straight and direct to the point. The manifestation of the gifts of healing was unquestionable. On those visits, I never discerned a contrary spirit in operation.

Hereunder is the statement of faith by SCOAN

https://www.scoan.org/about/statement-of-faith/

SCOAN Believe

The Holy Spirit worked with the Father and the Son to create the world. The Father gave His Spirit to make us like His Son, Jesus Christ. The Jesus Christ we know is Jesus in the power of the Holy Spirit. He made a wonderful promise in John 14:16-17: "I will ask the Father, and He will give you another Counselor to be with you forever — the Spirit of Truth. The world cannot accept Him, because it neither sees Him nor knows Him. But you know Him, for He lives with you and will be in you." The Holy Spirit is to be with us forever. He is not known or received by everyone, but only by those who are prepared for Him. The Holy Spirit shows us how wrong our sins are. He helps us to accept Jesus Christ as our Saviour. He completely changes our lives. This is called being converted or born again.

- Jesus Christ is a soul-winner. That is what He came for, lived for, died for and rose again for. He came to restore the relationship and fellowship between God and man. As to His human nature, Jesus Christ was a descendant of David. As to His divine nature, He was shown with great power to be the Son of God by being raised from death on the third day. Now He sits at the right hand of the throne of God (Hebrews 12:2; Romans 1:2-4). He was at all points tempted just as we are, yet was without sin. Jesus Christ loves us, died for us, reigns in power for us and still prays for us.

- Holy men of God were carried along by the Holy Spirit as they spoke the message that came from God. The Holy Bible is more than long-ago events and ancient wisdom. It is God's message of grace and truth to us today (2 Timothy 3:16; 2 Peter 1:21).
- Sin points one to eternal death and destruction but God's Word points one to life. If Christ Jesus is our Lord and Saviour, a new body, a new soul and a new spirit await us one day. God's Spirit joins Himself to our spirit to declare that we are God's children (Romans 8:16).
- Salvation is to be set free from sin and its penalties and is received by faith in the cleansing power of the Blood of Jesus Christ. Each man has to accept Jesus Christ as his personal Lord and Savior, otherwise Jesus' death will not save him.
- God's Word refreshes our minds while God's Spirit renews our strength. To be born again, not only must we have God's Word but also His Spirit, mixed with repentance and faith in our hearts.
- Divine healing is the supernatural power of God bringing health to the human body. It is received by faith in the finished work of our Lord Jesus Christ.

All the punishment Jesus Christ received before and during His crucifixion was for our healing – spirit, soul and body. By His stripes, we are healed. Divine healing was included in the benefits that Jesus Christ bought for us at Calvary.

- Water baptism and baptism in the Holy Spirit. We also believe in speaking in tongues as the Spirit of God gives utterance (Acts 2:4). All who enter into the number of the body of Christ do so because they are baptized in the Holy Spirit (1 Corinthians 12:13; Romans 8:9). When you are baptized in the Holy Spirit, God's power will come upon you as it did on the first disciples on the day of Pentecost (Acts 2:1-4). When God's power comes upon you, the Holy Spirit will affect everything about you. The Holy Spirit produces rivers of life, joy, love, peace and power to flow out of your spirit for the needs of others (John 7:37-38).

- The Lord's Supper as was celebrated by Jesus Christ and His disciples in Matthew 26:26-28,"While they were eating, Jesus took bread, gave thanks and broke it, and gave it to His disciples, saying, 'Take and eat; this is My body.' Then He took the cup, gave thanks and offered it to them, saying, 'Drink from it, all of you. This is My blood of the covenant, which is poured out for many for the forgiveness of sins.'" As the disciples of old were instructed to partake of the Lord's Supper by Jesus Christ, we also partake of the Lord's Supper (2 Peter 1:4), upon the instruction of the Holy Spirit (1 Corinthians 2:10; 11:26-31).

- Jesus Christ will come again, just as He went away (Acts 1:11; 1 Thessalonians. 4:16-17).

Some Raised Questions About Authenticity of Prophet T.B Joshua Based On Information The Heard About Him Prior. Hereunder Is Our Response In The Spirit Of Unity

I don't know about you but for me, my Christian race did not start on a smooth sailing. It took me years to figure out my stand in Christ and frankly speaking, I am still growing. Sometimes it is difficult for us, followers of Christ to articulate correctly the specific call of God over our lives. My call is to encourage unity of spirit by highlighting those things that holds us together and not those that divide. God in His infinite wisdom does not permit that all the gift of the spirit are present in one gathering so we can reach out to one another for the equipping of the saints and the work of ministry. Even if we do have all the gifts, they are usually in varying measure. Benny Hinn once fell ill and needed another pastor to lay hands on Him before he got his healing. Believers had to call on Peter in the book of Acts 9:36-43 to restore Dorcas, the disciple back to life. In summary when I am confused on the authenticity of a man of God, I would look out for the fruit as Jesus instructed. Check the scriptures to help clarity and also how Jesus responded to a man using His name to cast out demons..

Conclusion

What I cannot understand, till date is why we create unnecessary problems for ourselves by segregating ourselves into denominations with no Jesus foundation. God is love, love permits diversity in unity - Love is the only clue that can hold us together. Don't we realize that even if we have 7 billion members, the work of ministry cannot be completed by one ministry? Our disunity is delaying the return of our lord and savior Jesus Christ because many, seeing our disunity will not come to the Lord. Let us open channels of communication with each other and let us do it now. Take time to read, in meditative mode, John 17, the prayer Jesus prayed for me and you believers and remain united.

Prayer

Dear Lord God, we present Your body of believers around the world before You today, Lord, help us to let go of petty differences and focus on the high calling of God for our lives. Help us to accommodate each other in love. Help us to be reconciled to You and to one another despite our diversity in Jesus name I have prayed (Amen)

Shalom!

Monday Ogwuojo Ogbe – E-discipleship @

Shalom!

Chapter 18 - The Christian Church – What Is The Nicene Creed, Where Did The Nicene Creed Come From And What Are The Interpretation Of Each Declaration? When Values Or Creeds Don't Agree Or Align, How Did Jesus And The Early Disciples Engaged Them?

Introduction

We are looking at the Nicene Creed – What is it? What brought it about?

Also, we would look at Jesus and the early disciples' response to those who do not share the same values with them so we can learn in our day and age and apply without losing sight of our values, believes and going out to make disciples of ALL Nations. Our objective is to shed light on what unites us in the various Christian groups so that we can begin to engage from our closets and on the frontlines thereby making us more proactive and precise in our intercession for the body of Christ for the call to unity of Spirit just as Christ prayed in John 17

Key verses

Luke 4:14-30 ¹⁴ Then Jesus went back to Galilee in the power of the Spirit, and the news about Him spread through the entire region. ¹⁵ And He *began* teaching in their synagogues and was
praised *and* glorified *and* honored by all.
¹⁶ So He came to Nazareth, where He had been brought up; and as was His custom, He entered the synagogue on the Sabbath, and stood up to read. ¹⁷ The scroll of the prophet Isaiah was handed to Him. He unrolled the scroll and found the place where it was written,
¹⁸

"The Spirit of the Lord is upon Me (the Messiah),
Because He has anointed Me to preach the good news to the poor.
He has sent Me to announce release (pardon,

forgiveness) to the captives,

And recovery of sight to the blind,

To set free those who are oppressed (downtrodden, bruised, crushed by tragedy),

¹⁹ to proclaim the favorable year of the Lord [the day when salvation and the favor of God abound greatly]."

²⁰ Then He rolled up the scroll [having stopped in the middle of the verse], gave it back to the attendant and sat down [to teach]; and the eyes of all those in the synagogue were [attentively] fixed on Him. ²¹ He began speaking to them: "Today this Scripture has been fulfilled in your hearing *and* in your presence." ²² And [as He continued on] they all were speaking well of Him, and were in awe *and* were wondering about the words of grace which were coming from His lips; and they were saying, "Is this not Joseph's son?" ²³ So He said to them, "You will no doubt quote this proverb to Me, 'Physician, heal Yourself! Whatever [miracles] that we heard were done [by You] in Capernaum, do here in Your hometown as well.'"²⁴ Then He said, "I assure you *and* most solemnly say to you, no prophet is welcome in his hometown. ²⁵ But in truth I say to you, there were many widows in Israel in the days of Elijah, when the sky was closed up for three years and six months, when a great famine came over all the land; ²⁶ and yet Elijah was not sent[by the Lord] to a single one of them, but only to Zarephath *in the land* of Sidon, to a woman who was a widow. ²⁷ And there were many lepers in Israel in the time of Elisha the prophet; and not one of them was cleansed [by being healed] except Naaman the Syrian." ²⁸ As they heard these things [about God's grace to these two Gentiles], *the people* in the synagogue were filled with a great rage; ²⁹ and they got up and drove Him out of the city, and led Him to the crest of the hill on which

their city had been built, in order to hurl Him down the cliff. ³⁰ But passing [miraculously] through the crowd, He went on His way.

Matthew 4:23
[*Ministry in Galilee*] **And** He **went** throughout all Galilee, **teaching** in their synagogues **and preaching** the good news (gospel) of the kingdom, **and** healing every kind of disease **and** every kind of sickness among the people [demonstrating **and** revealing that He was indeed the promised Messiah].

Matthew 9:34
But the **Pharisees** were saying, "He casts out the demons by [the power of] the ruler of demons."

Matthew 16:1
[*Pharisees* Test Jesus] Now the **Pharisees** and Sadducees came up, and testing Jesus [to get something to use against Him], they asked Him to show them a sign from heaven [which would support His divine authority].

Matthew 12:14
But the **Pharisees** went out and conspired against Him, *discussing* how they could destroy Him.

Mark 6:2
When the Sabbath came, He began to teach in the **synagogue**; and many who listened to Him were astonished, saying, "Where did this man get these things [this knowledge and spiritual insight]? What is this wisdom [this confident understanding of the Scripture] that has been given to Him, and such miracles as these performed by His hands?

Act 4:1-4 And while Peter and John were talking to the people, the priests and the captain [who was in charge of the temple area and] of the temple *guard* and the Sadducees came up to them, [2] being extremely disturbed *and* thoroughly annoyed because they were teaching the people and proclaiming in [the case of] Jesus the resurrection of the dead. [3] So they arrested them and put them in jail until the next day, because it was evening. [4] But many of those who heard the message [of salvation] believed [in Jesus and accepted Him as the Christ]. And the number of the men came to be about 5,000.

Acts 13:5
When Barnabas and Saul arrived at Salamis, they *began* to preach the word of God [proclaiming the message of eternal salvation through faith in Christ] in the **synagogue**s of the Jews; and they also had John [Mark] as their assistant.

Acts 17:2
And Paul entered the **synagogue**, as was his custom, and for three Sabbaths he engaged in discussion *and* friendly debate with them from the Scriptures,

What is the Nicene Creed, Where did the Nicene Creed come?

The Nicene Creed is the declaration of the Christian faith for all Catholics and Orthodox as well as many Protestants. It is also called the Niceno-Constantinopolitan Creed, because it was defined at the Councils of Nicaea (325 A.D.) and Constantinople (381 A.D.).

The Nicene Creed explains the Church's teachings about the Trinity and affirms historical realities of Jesus' life. The creed does not directly quote Scripture, but it is based on biblical truths.

The Council of Nicaea was the first general council of the Church since the Apostolic Council of Jerusalem, which set conditions for Gentiles to join the Church. Roman persecution of Christians had just ended 12 years earlier, but now the Church was divided over the question of Jesus' divinity. Heretics led by a priest named Arius in Alexandria, Egypt, claimed that if Jesus was begotten by God, He must have had a beginning like every other part of God's creation – therefore, Jesus was not fully God.

The theological dispute threatened the peace of the Roman empire, so Emperor Constantine – at the request of several concerned bishops – called for a meeting of all the Church's bishops in the easily accessible town of Nicaea (present-day Iznik, Turkey), organized like the Roman Senate with himself as a non-voting observer. The council met in Senatus Palace (which now lies under Lake Iznik).

An estimated 318 bishops came from Rome, Jerusalem and Palestine, Egypt, Syria, Greece, Asia Minor, Persia, Georgia, Armenia, Gaul, Hispania and the Danube. Among them were Pope St. Silvester, St. Nicholas of Myra, St. Eusebius of Caesarea (considered the Church's first historian), St. Athanasius and St. Alexander of Alexandria. Each bishop could bring up to two priests and three deacons, so the total attendance could have been as many as 1,800.

Many of the bishops had the marks of persecution on their faces – they had faced the threat of death for their faith and they were sensitive to details of doctrine. These were not wishy-washy men.

The council's main purpose was to quash the Arian heresy and settle the doctrine of the Trinity – that God, Jesus and the Holy Spirit were three divine persons in complete union. The term "Trinity" was not new, of course. Besides Jesus' references to it in Scripture, many early Church fathers had written about it from the 1st century onward.

Besides the Arian heresy, the council fathers wanted to settle the date for celebrating Easter, and they had to contend with various practical problems such as usury and self-castration.

On May 20, 325, the council opened. It is likely they had a draft from Bishop Hosius of Cordova to consider, as several creeds were already in use by Christians to identify themselves, and as a means of inclusion and recognition, especially at baptism. In Rome, for example, the Apostles' Creed was popular.

After being in session for an entire month, the council promulgated on June 19 the original Nicene Creed, written in Greek. All but two of the bishops, who were Arian sympathizers, approved the text. Those two bishops, as well as Arius, were excommunicated and exiled.

Besides the creed, the council decided that the date for Easter should be calculated uniformly and separate from the Jewish calendar, using the lunar calendar instead. But it took centuries for the calculations to be worked out in practice, and disagreement remains between Catholics in the West and Orthodox in the East.

The council also promulgated 20 new church laws, called canons. These included: prohibiting self-castration (which some had thought was a path to greater holiness), prohibiting young women from entering a cleric's home; requiring bishops to be ordained in the presence of at least three other bishops; prohibiting the removal of priests; forbidding usury among the clergy; determining the order of bishops, then priests, then deacons receiving Holy Communion; declaring invalid any baptisms done by heretics; acknowledging the special authority of the patriarchs of Rome, Alexandria and Antioch in their respective regions; and setting a minimum time frame for catechumens to prepare for baptism.

The long-term effects of the Council of Nicaea were significant. For the first time, leaders of the Church convened to agree on a doctrinal statement. In the short term, however, the council did not stamp out the heresy it was convened to discuss, and upheaval continued for some time even after Arius himself died.

It was only a few years after the Council of Nicaea that Arius returned to Constantinople and asked to be readmitted to the Church. But Arius did not renounce his heresy, so the Church refused. Emperor Constantine intervened in the dispute, setting a date for Arius to attend Mass and be forcibly readmitted to Communion. While he was waiting for Constantine to arrive so he could go into Mass, Arius stopped to relieve himself. His bowels burst out of his body, and he died instantly.

The Nicene Creed did not become a part of Mass until the early 6th century, when Patriarch Timothy of Constantinople started the practice to combat heresy. Its popularity spread throughout the Byzantine Empire, then to Spain, France and northern Europe. In 1114 Emperor Henry II, who had come to Rome for his coronation as Holy Roman Emperor, was surprised that they did not recite the creed. He was told that since Rome had never erred in matters of faith there was no need for the Romans to proclaim it at Mass. However, it was included in deference to the new emperor and has pretty much remained ever since – not at daily Mass, but on Sundays and feast days.

The Nicene Creed expressed what the early leaders of the Church found to be Biblical, traditional and orthodox in their Christian faith – a faith in Jesus Christ that we continue to proclaim 1,700 years later.

What is the interpretation of each declaration line?

I BELIEVE IN ONE GOD

Christians, like Jews and Muslims, believe that only one God exists. The creed states the assumption of the ancient Shema: "Hear O Israel, the Lord our God is one Lord." It begins with "I believe," because reciting the creed is ultimately an individual confession of belief, although the creed also expresses the collective beliefs of the Church.

THE FATHER ALMIGHTY

Jesus frequently calls God "Father" in the Scriptures, and this usage tells us that God is a loving God active within His creation. God the Father is the first person (Greek "hypostasis," "individual reality"), or distinction, within the Godhead. The Father is the "origin" or "source" of the Trinity. As such, God the Father is often called "God Unbegotten" in early Christian thought.

MAKER OF HEAVEN AND EARTH, OF ALL THINGS VISIBLE AND INVISIBLE

The Christian church believe that God created the visible world (created matter) and the invisible one (spiritual world of angels, etc.). Thus, God created everything. Some early sects, such as the Gnostics, believed that God the Father created the spirit world, but that an "evil" god (called the "demiurge") created the similarly evil material world. The creed dispels such a notion.

I BELIEVE IN ONE LORD JESUS CHRIST

Jesus Christ is the Lord of all. The title Lord means that Jesus is master of all, and has connotations of deity, since the Hebrew word "adonai" and Greek word "kyrios" (both meaning Lord) were applied to Yahweh in the Old Testament. However, unlike earthly rulers, Jesus is a friend to the oppressed and a servant.

THE ONLY BEGOTTEN SON OF GOD

Jesus is in a unique relationship with God the Father. While Hebrew kings were sons of God symbolically (see Psalm 2), Jesus is the only Son of God by nature.

BORN OF THE FATHER BEFORE ALL AGES

Begotten has the meaning of born, generated, or produced. God the Son is born out of the essence of God the Father. Just as a child shares the same humanness as his or her parents, the Son shares the essential nature of God with the Father. Since God is eternal, the Son, being begotten of God, is also eternal.

GOD FROM GOD, LIGHT FROM LIGHT

God the Son exists in relation to God the Father. The Son is not the Father, but they both are God. Just as a torch is lit one to another, the Father and Son are distinct, but both light. Some Christians, called Sabellians or Modalists, wrongly said that the Father, Son, and Holy Spirit were one God who changes roles. So when God creates, He is Father, while on earth, He is Son, and so forth. However, the Scriptures have all three persons – Father, Son, and Holy Spirit – interacting at the same time, as shown at Jesus' baptism. St. Athanasius, writing during the Nicene era, said the Father and Son are one as "the sight of two eyes is one."

TRUE GOD FROM TRUE GOD

God the Son is not a half-god or inferior to God the Father. God the Son is fully and utterly God, distinct from the Father, yet not divided from the Father. The Arians said Jesus could be called god but not true God. In other words, they wrongly believed the Logos (the "Word," a popular title for Jesus in early Christian literature) was the first creation of God.

BEGOTTEN, NOT MADE

Some Christians today (Jehovah's Witnesses) and in the past (Arians) have suggested God created Jesus like God would an angel. The creed tells us that just as when a woman gives birth she does not create a child out of nothing, being begotten of God, the Son is not created out of nothing. Since the Son's birth from the Father occurred before time was created, begotten refers to a permanent relationship as opposed to an event within time.

CONSUBSTANTIAL WITH THE FATHER

God the Father and God the Son are equally divine, united in substance and will. Father and Son share the same substance or essence of divinity. That is, the Father and Son both share the qualities and essential nature that make one in reality God. However, sharing the same substance does not mean they share identity of person.

THROUGH HIM ALL THINGS WERE MADE

The Bible tells us that through the Son, as Word of God, all things have been created.

FOR US MEN AND FOR OUR SALVATION, HE CAME DOWN FROM HEAVEN

Jesus came from heaven, from a spiritual reality other than our own. While the creed says "down," it is important to remember that our language is limited by time and spatiality. Heaven is not "up," just as God is not a biologically male father.

AND BY THE HOLY SPIRIT, WAS INCARNATE OF THE VIRGIN MARY, AND BECAME MAN

God the Son became incarnate in the person of Jesus of Nazareth. He was born of a virgin through the Holy Spirit. God truly became human in Jesus Christ. Catholics believe that Jesus of Nazareth was and is a real human being, not simply a spirit or ghost. The incarnation of God in Christ is the ultimate act of love, because rather than sending an angel or good human to accomplish the redemption and restoration of creation, God Himself became human.

FOR OUR SAKE HE WAS CRUCIFIED UNDER PONTIUS PILATE; HE SUFFERED DEATH AND WAS BURIED

Jesus died on a cross, suffered as humans do, truly died, and was laid in a tomb. Despite what some critics will level against it, the Nicene Creed is more than just metaphysical speculation, and includes important historical confessions. Notice that in addition to being "true God from true God," Jesus is fully human as well. The early Docetists, named from the Greek word "dokeo" ("to seem"), heretically believed Jesus only seemed to be human, but was not.

AND ROSE AGAIN ON THE THIRD DAY IN ACCORDANCE WITH THE SCRIPTURES

Jesus was resurrected bodily, as the Scriptures say. Just as Jesus truly died, He truly rose from the dead three days later. The bodily resurrection is the keystone of Christian doctrine and experience. However, Jesus was not just physically resuscitated (as was Lazarus), but rather His body was transformed at the Resurrection. The word "again" is used because Jesus' first "rising" was His birth. To "rise again" is be alive again.

HE ASCENDED INTO HEAVEN AND IS SEATED AT THE RIGHT HAND OF THE FATHER

In ancient science, heaven was thought to be situated above the sky dome. So in the Scriptures, Jesus is said to ascend to heaven. Whatever happened that day, Luke had to render the event into his own scientific paradigm, so he said Jesus "went up" to heaven.

HE WILL COME AGAIN IN GLORY TO JUDGE THE LIVING AND THE DEAD, AND HIS KINGDOM WILL HAVE NO END

Jesus is coming again to righteously judge the living and dead. His kingdom cannot be destroyed, despite all of humanity's efforts. The creed says Jesus is coming; it does not say when or how, nor does it say to speculate on the date of His return.

I BELIEVE IN THE HOLY SPIRIT, THE LORD, THE GIVER OF LIFE

The Holy Spirit is also called "Lord." The Holy Spirit sustains our lives as Christians, illuminating us after the new birth. The original Creed of Nicaea simply ended with "We believe in the Holy Spirit." The other additions were approved at the Council of Constantinople in 381 A.D. However, most scholars believe that the text of the full creed dates prior to this council, and that the bishops simply gave their approval to a local creed already in use. The reason these additions were included in the Nicene

Creed is that some heretics of the 4th century denied the full divinity of the Holy Spirit.

WHO PROCEEDS FROM THE FATHER AND THE SON

The Son is said to be begotten, while the Spirit is said to proceed. Both words convey that the Son and Spirit are in special relationships to the Father, yet also fully divine. The phrase "and the Son" (in Latin, "filioque,") was not in the original text of the creed, but was added in many Western Churches in the late 6th century. The addition likely developed over time as a tool against Arianism. There are theological and historical justifications for the addition or exclusion of the filioque. The Eastern Churches oppose the addition of the filioque, while many Western churches accept it. Actually, despite current division on the matter, the issue has been pretty much theologically resolved.

WHO WITH THE FATHER AND THE SON IS ADORED AND GLORIFIED

The Holy Spirit is God as are the Father and the Son, and worthy of the same worship.

WHO HAS SPOKEN THROUGH THE PROPHETS

The Spirit inspired the prophets of old and inspires the Church today.

I BELIEVE IN ONE, HOLY, CATHOLIC AND APOSTOLIC CHURCH

The creed requires belief in the Catholic (universal) Church, whose origins go back to the Apostles themselves. The Church is "holy" on account of Christ's holiness and grace, and not because its members or leaders are perfect. In fact, at times throughout history, the Church has remained holy in spite of its members.

I CONFESS ONE BAPTISM FOR THE FORGIVENESS OF SINS

This belief is universally acknowledged in early Christian writings. If someone has been validly baptized in the name of the Trinity, re-baptism is unnecessary.

AND I LOOK FORWARD TO THE RESURRECTION OF THE DEAD, AND THE LIFE OF THE WORLD TO COME. AMEN.

Christians always hope for the end of this fractured system, when the universe is fully reconciled to God in Christ Jesus. The Nicene Creed affirms both the existence of a soul-filled heaven and the later resurrection of the dead when soul meets glorified body.

Conclusion and Prayer

Jesus Christ, our Lord and Savior engaged on all fronts.. preached and taught in the synagogue, debated in the synagogue, casted out demons in the synagogues and on the streets, engaged with sinners, despite opposition and attack on His life even in the synagogues, He continued to engaged them, pushing His agenda on all fronts until He was crucified. You would have thought the disciples will flee the synagogues because of what they did to their master, but no, the gospel of Jesus Christ was not something to be hidden from anyone including the opposition whom the enemy has blinded their eyes. They disciples went on the offensive, preaching and teaching in the synagogues and on the street and in homes. Paul preached, debated, was persecuted in the synagogue but these did not deter him. How can we be effective in pushing the agenda of Christ in our day and age if we do not step out of the four walls of our cute churches, of our creeds, our values and engage on all fronts? May the Lord open our hearts and minds to receive what is in the mind of the Spirit in our day and age in Jesus name, Amen

Shalom!

Chapter 19 - The Christian Church – Searchlight On The Evangelicals – Part 7

Introduction

We are looking at the evangelical Christians – evangelical Christianity, or evangelical Protestantism, is a worldwide, trans-denominational movement within Protestant Christianity which maintains the belief that the essence of the Gospel consists of the doctrine of salvation by grace through faith in Jesus Christ's atonement.. It is imperative to clarify at the outset about the word "evangelical." Since Pentecostals generally are evangelicals. There are "conservative evangelicalism" which "generally refers to that portion of evangelicalism that is *non-charismatic.*

Key verses

1 Corinthians 1:10-15 New Living Translation

[10] But, dear brothers, I beg you in the name of the Lord Jesus Christ to stop arguing among yourselves. Let there be real harmony so that there won't be splits in the church. I plead with you to be of one mind, united in thought and purpose. [11] For some of those who live at Chloe's house have told me of your arguments and quarrels, dear brothers. [12] Some of you are saying, "I am a follower of Paul"; and others say that they are for Apollos or for Peter; and some that they alone are the true followers of Christ. **[13] And so, in effect, you have broken Christ into many pieces.**

But did I, Paul, die for your sins? Were any of you baptized in my name? [14] I am so thankful now that I didn't baptize any of you except Crispus and Gaius. [15] For now no one can think that I have been trying to start something new, beginning a "Church of Paul."

2 Kings 6:17-20 New International Version (NIV)
[17] And Elisha prayed, "Open his eyes, Lord, so that he may see." Then the Lord opened the servant's eyes, and he looked and saw the hills full of horses and chariots of fire all around Elisha.
[18] As the enemy came down toward him, Elisha prayed to the Lord, "Strike this army with blindness." So he struck them with blindness, as Elisha had asked.
[19] Elisha told them, "This is not the road and this is not the city. Follow me, and I will lead you to the man you are looking for." And he led them to Samaria.
[20] After they entered the city, Elisha said, "Lord, open the eyes of these men so they can see." Then the Lord opened their eyes and they looked, and there they were, inside Samaria.

Searchlight: – What Evangelical Christians Believe

Evangelicals believe that the Bible is the Word of God; without error as originally written. Its content has been preserved by Him, and is the final authority in all matters of doctrine and faith-above all human authority.**Scriptural references:(Isa 40:8)** The grass withereth, the flower fadeth: but the word of our God shall stand for ever.**(Psalm 12:6-7)** The words of the LORD are pure words: as silver tried in a furnace of earth, purified seven times. Thou shalt keep them, O LORD, thou shalt preserve them from this generation for ever.(Psalm 18:30) As for God, his way is perfect: the word of the LORD is tried: he is a buckler to all those that trust in him.**(Psalm 119:105)** Thy word is a lamp unto my feet, and a light unto my path.

Scriptural references

(Psalm 119:160) Thy word is true from the beginning: and every one of thy righteous judgments endureth for ever.
(Matt 5:18) For verily I say unto you, Till heaven and earth pass, one jot or one tittle shall in no wise pass from the law, till all be fulfilled.
(Matt 24:35) Heaven and earth shall pass away, but my words shall not pass away.
(John 17:17) Sanctify them through thy truth: thy word is truth.
(2Tim 3:16) All scripture is given by inspiration of God, and is profitable for doctrine, for reproof, for correction, for instruction in righteousness:
(Heb 4:12) For the word of God is quick, and powerful, and sharper than any twoedged sword, piercing even to the dividing asunder of soul and spirit, and of the joints and marrow, and is a discerner of the thoughts and intents of the heart.
(2Pet 1:20-21) Knowing this first, that no prophecy of the scripture is of any private interpretation. For the prophecy came not in old time by the will of man: but holy men of God spake as they were moved by the Holy Ghost.
(2Pet 3:15-16) ...as our beloved brother Paul also according to the wisdom given unto him hath written unto you; As also in all his epistles, speaking in them of these things; in which are some things hard to be understood,

which they that are unlearned and unstable wrest, as they do <u>also the other scriptures</u>, unto their own destruction.

God. We believe there is no God but *one*: the infinite Designer, Creator, and Sustainer of all existence in this or any universe-from eternity past to eternity future. God's nature is triune-three perfect and eternal persons; Father, Son, and Holy Spirit-who are *one*, in being as well as in purpose.

Scriptural Reference

(Gen 1:1) In the beginning God created the heaven and the earth.
(Exod 3:13-15) And Moses said unto God, Behold, when I come unto the children of Israel, and shall say unto them, The God of your fathers hath sent me unto you; and they shall say to me, What is his name? what shall I say unto them? And God said unto Moses, I AM THAT I AM: and he said, Thus shalt thou say unto the children of Israel, I AM* hath sent me unto you. ...this is my name for ever, and this is my memorial unto all generations.
[* *Literally: Existence*]

(Psalm 8:3) When I consider thy heavens, the work of thy fingers, the moon and the stars, which thou hast ordained;

(Psalm 147:4-5) He telleth the number of the stars; he calleth them all by their names. Great is our Lord, and of great power: his understanding is infinite.

(Deut 6:4) Hear, O Israel: The LORD our God is one LORD:

(1Kgs 8:60) That all the people of the earth may know that the LORD is God, and that there is none else.

(Psalm 90:2) Before the mountains were brought forth, or ever thou hadst formed the earth and the world, even from everlasting to everlasting, thou art God.

(Isa 43:10-11) Ye are my witnesses, saith the LORD, and my servant whom I have chosen: that ye may know and believe me, and understand that I am he: before me there was no God formed, neither shall there be after me. I, even I, am the LORD; and beside me there is no saviour.

(Isa 44:6) Thus saith the LORD the King of Israel, and his redeemer the LORD of hosts; I am the first, and I am the last; and beside me there is no God.

(Isa 44:8) Fear ye not, neither be afraid: have not I told thee from that time, and have declared it? ye are even my witnesses. Is there a God beside me? yea, there is no God; I know not any.

(Isa 45:5) I am the LORD, and there is none else, there is no God beside me: I girded thee, though thou hast not known me: That they may know from the rising of the sun, and from the west, that there is none beside me. I am the LORD, and there is none else.

(John 1:1-3) In the beginning was the Word, and the Word was with God, and the Word was God. The same was in the beginning with God. All things were made** by him; and without him was not any thing made** that was made**.

[**Greek *ginomai: to cause to be, or bring into existence. Thus "All things were brought into existence by him; and without him nothing was brought into existence that exists."*]

(John 8:23-24) And he said unto them, Ye are from beneath; I am from above: ye are of this world; I am not of this world. I said therefore unto you, that ye shall die in your sins: for if ye believe not that I am *he****, ye shall die in your sins.

[****The italicized word "he" is not actually present in the Greek text but is usually an implied word with this syntax. The later context in John 8:58 suggests that "he" should be omitted here, although His audience would have initially been likewise confused. Thus: "If ye believe not that I AM, ye shall die in your sins."*]

(John 10:30) I and my Father are one.

(Col 1:16-19) For by him were all things created, that are in heaven, and that are in earth, visible and invisible, whether they be thrones, or dominions, or principalities, or powers: all things were created by him, and for him: and he is before all things, and <u>by him all things consist</u>. and he is the head of the body, the church: who is the beginning, the firstborn from the dead; that in all things he might have the preeminence. For it pleased the Father that in him should all fulness dwell

(Col 2:9) For in him dwelleth all the fulness of the Godhead bodily.

(Titus 3:4) But after that the kindness and love of <u>God our Saviour</u> toward man appeared...

(Heb 1:1-3) God, who at sundry times and in divers manners spake in time past unto the fathers by the prophets, hath in these last days spoken unto us by his Son, whom he hath appointed heir of all things, by whom also he made the worlds; who being the brightness of his glory, and the express image of his person, and <u>upholding all things by the word of his power</u>, when he had by himself purged our sins, sat down on the right hand of the Majesty on high

(Acts 5:3-4) But Peter said, Ananias, why hath Satan filled thine heart to lie to the <u>Holy Ghost</u>, and to keep back part of the price of the land? Whiles it remained, was it not thine own? and after it was sold, was it not in thine own power? why hast thou conceived this thing in thine heart? thou hast not lied unto men, but unto <u>God</u>.

(John 15:26) But when the Comforter is come, whom I will send unto you from the Father, even the Spirit of truth, which proceedeth from the Father, he shall testify of me:

(Matt 28:19) Go ye therefore, and teach all nations, baptizing them in the name of the Father, and of the Son, and of the Holy Ghost

(1John 5:7) For there are three that bear record in heaven, the Father,

Law. We believe God is the source of all moral and natural law. The highest and all-encompassing law, given to man, is to love the one *true* God above all else.

Scriptural references

(James 4:12) There is one lawgiver, who is able to save and to destroy: who art thou that judgest another?

(Psalm 148:5-6) Let them praise the name of the LORD: for he commanded, and they were created. He hath also stablished them for ever and ever: he hath made a decree which shall not pass.

(Gen 1:3) And God said, Let there be light: and there was light.

(Job 38:4) Where wast thou when I laid the foundations of the earth? declare, if thou hast understanding.

(Matt 22:36-40) Master, which is the great commandment in the law? Jesus said unto him, Thou shalt love the Lord thy God with all thy heart, and with all thy soul, and with all thy mind. This is the first and great commandment. And the second is like unto it, Thou shalt love thy neighbour as thyself. On these two commandments hang all the law and the prophets.

(Deut 6:4-9) Hear, O Israel: The LORD our God is one LORD: And thou shalt love the LORD thy God with all thine heart, and with all thy soul, and with all thy might. And these words, which I command thee this day, shall be in thine heart: And thou shalt teach them diligently unto thy children, and shalt talk of them when thou sittest in thine house, and when thou walkest by the way, and when thou liest down, and when thou risest up. And thou shalt bind them for a sign upon thine hand, and they shall be as frontlets between thine eyes. And thou shalt write them upon the posts of thy house, and on thy gates.
(Exodus 34:14) For thou shalt worship no other god: for the LORD, whose name is Jealous, is a jealous God:
(Deut 4:24) For the LORD thy God is a consuming fire, even a jealous God.
(Exod 20:3) Thou shalt have no other gods before me.

Man. We believe that man is a *created*, finite being; designed in the image of God, with the ability to reason, make choices, and have relationships. Man was created for the purpose of bringing glory to God, but since the day man first rebelled against God's law, all mankind has been sinful by nature, and has earned the penalty of death and eternal separation from God

Scriptural references
(Gen 1:26-27) And God said, Let us make man in our image, after our likeness: and let them have dominion over the fish of the sea, and over the fowl of the air, and over the cattle, and over all the earth, and over every creeping thing that creepeth upon the earth. So God

created man in his own image, in the image of God created he him; male and female created he them.

(Gen 2:7,25) And the LORD God formed man of the dust of the ground, and breathed into his nostrils the breath of life; and man became a living soul... And they were both naked, the man and his wife, and were not ashamed.

(Gen 3:12-13) And the man said, The woman whom thou gavest to be with me, she gave me of the tree, and I did eat. And the LORD God said unto the woman, What is this that thou hast done? And the woman said, The serpent beguiled me, and I did eat.

(Prov 14:12) There is a way which seemeth right unto a man, but the end thereof are the ways of death.

(Isa 43:1,7) But now thus saith the LORD that created thee, O Jacob, and he that formed thee, O Israel, Fear not: for I have redeemed thee, I have called thee by thy name; thou art mine... Even every one that is called by my name: for I have created him for my glory, I have formed him; yea, I have made him.

(Isa 64:6) But we are all as an unclean thing, and all our righteousnesses are as filthy rags; and we all do fade as a leaf; and our iniquities, like the wind, have taken us away.

(Ezek 18:4) Behold, all souls are mine; as the soul of the father, so also the soul of the son is mine: the soul that sinneth, it shall die.

(Eccl 7:29) Lo, this only have I found, that God hath made man upright; but they have sought out many inventions.

(Matt 13:41-42) The Son of man shall send forth his angels, and they shall gather out of his kingdom all things that offend, and them which do iniquity; And shall cast them into a furnace of fire: there shall be wailing and gnashing of teeth.

(Rom 3:10, 19-20, 23) As it is written, There is none righteous, no, not one... Now we know that what things soever the law saith, it saith to them who are under the law: that every mouth may be stopped, and all the world may become guilty before God. Therefore by the deeds of the law there shall no flesh be justified in his sight: for by the law is the knowledge of sin... For all have sinned, and come short of the glory of God;

(Rom 5:12-19) Wherefore, as by one man sin entered into the world, and death by sin; and so death passed upon all men, for that all have sinned: (For until the law sin was in the world: but sin is not imputed when there is no law. Nevertheless death reigned from Adam to Moses, even over them that had not sinned after the similitude of Adam's transgression, who is the figure of him that was to come. But not as the offence, so also is the free gift. For if through the offence of one many be dead, much more the grace of God, and the gift by grace, which is by one man, Jesus Christ, hath abounded unto many. And not as it was by one that sinned, so is the gift: for the judgment was by one to condemnation, but the free gift is of many offences unto justification. For if by one man's offence death reigned by one; much more they which receive abundance of grace and of the gift of righteousness shall reign in life by one, Jesus Christ.) Therefore as by the offence of one judgment came upon all men to condemnation; even so by the righteousness of one the free gift came upon all men unto justification of life. For as by one man's disobedience many were made sinners, so by the obedience of one shall many be made righteous.
(Rom 6:23) For the wages of sin is death; but the gift of God is eternal life through Jesus Christ our Lord.

(1Cor 15:22) For as in Adam all die, even so in Christ shall all be made alive.

(Eph 2:1-2) And you hath he quickened, who were <u>dead in trespasses and sins</u>; Wherein in time past ye walked according to the course of this world, according to the prince of the power of the air, the spirit that now worketh in the children of disobedience:
(Matt 7:22-23) Many will say to me in that day, Lord, Lord, have we not prophesied in thy name? and in thy name have cast out devils? and in thy name done many wonderful works? And then will I profess unto them, <u>I never knew you</u>: depart from me, ye that work iniquity.
(John 17:3) And this is life eternal, that they might know thee the only true God, and Jesus Christ, whom thou hast sent.
(Phil 3:8) Yea doubtless, and I count all things but loss for the excellency of the <u>knowledge of Christ Jesus my Lord</u>: for whom I have suffered the loss of all things, and do count them but dung, that I may win Christ,
(Jas 2:10) For whosoever shall keep the whole law, and yet offend in one point, he is guilty of all.
(Rev 20:12,15) And I saw the dead, small and great, stand before God; and the books were opened: and another book was opened, which is the book of life: and the dead were judged out of those

Jesus. We believe that God, the Son, entered the world as a man to die on the cross on our behalf; a sinless sacrifice in full payment of all our sin-both past and future-satisfying the demand of God's perfect justice. Jesus rose from the grave; authenticating His divine identity, as our *living* Prophet, Priest, and King.

Scriptural References

(John 1:1-3,14) In the beginning was the Word, and the Word was with God, and the Word was God. The same was in the beginning with God. All things were made by him; and without him was not anything made that was made... And the Word was made flesh, and dwelt among us, (and we beheld his glory, the glory as of the only begotten of the Father,) full of grace and truth.
(Isa 9:6) For unto us a child is born, unto us a son is given: and the government shall be upon his shoulder: and his name shall be called Wonderful, Counsellor, The mighty God, The everlasting Father, The Prince of Peace.

(Matt 1:21-23) And she shall bring forth a son, and thou shalt call his name JESUS: for he shall save his people from their sins. Now all this was done, that it might be fulfilled which was spoken of the Lord by the prophet,
saying, **Behold, a virgin shall be with child, and shall bring forth a son, and they shall call his name Emmanuel,** which being interpreted is, God with us.
(John 3:13) And no man hath ascended up to heaven, but he that came down from heaven, even the Son of man which is in heaven.

(Rom 1:3-4) Concerning his Son Jesus Christ our Lord, which was made of the seed of David according to the flesh; And declared to be the Son of God with power, according to the spirit of holiness, by the resurrection from the dead
(1Cor 15:3-4) For I delivered unto you first of all that which I also received, how that Christ died for our sins according to the scriptures; And that he was buried, and that he rose again the third day according to the scriptures:

(John 19:30) When Jesus therefore had received the vinegar, he said, It is finished: [*literally the debt is discharged*] and he bowed his head, and gave up the ghost.

(2Cor 5:21) For he hath made him to be sin for us, who knew no sin; that we might be made the righteousness of God in him.

(Col 2:13-14) And you, being dead in your sins and the uncircumcision of your flesh, hath he quickened together with him, having forgiven you all trespasses; Blotting out the handwriting of ordinances that was against us, which was contrary to us, and took it out of the way, nailing it to his cross;

(Rom 3:25-26) Whom God hath set forth to be a propitiation through faith in his blood, to declare his righteousness for the remission of sins that are past, through the forbearance of God; To declare, I say, at this time his righteousness: that he might be just, and the justifier of him which believeth in Jesus.

(Isa 53:1011) Yet it pleased the LORD to bruise him; he hath put him to grief: when thou shalt make his soul an offering for sin, he shall see his seed, he shall prolong his days, and the pleasure of the LORD shall prosper in his hand. He shall see of the travail of his soul, and shall be satisfied: by his knowledge shall my righteous servant justify many; for he shall bear their iniquities.

(Heb 10:10,14,18) By the which will we are sanctified through the offering of the body of Jesus Christ once for all... For by one offering he hath perfected for ever them that are sanctified... Now where remission of these is, there is no more offering for sin.

Prophet

(Deut 18:15) The LORD thy God will raise up unto thee a Prophet from the midst of thee, of thy brethren, like unto me [*Moses*]; unto him ye shall hearken;

(Heb 1:1-3) God, who at sundry times and in divers manners spake in time past unto the fathers by the prophets, Hath in these last days spoken unto us by his Son, whom he hath appointed heir of all things, by whom also he made the worlds; Who being the brightness of his glory, and the express image of his person, and upholding all things by the word of his power, when he had by himself purged our sins, sat down on the right hand of the Majesty on high

Priest

(Heb 4:14-15) Seeing then that we have a great high priest, that is passed into the heavens, Jesus the Son of God, let us hold fast our profession. For we have not an high priest which cannot be touched with the feeling of our infirmities; but was in all points tempted like as we are, yet without sin.

(Heb 7:15-17,22-25) And it is yet far more evident: for that after the similitude of Melchisedec there ariseth another priest, who is made, not after the law of a carnal commandment, but after the power of an endless life. For he testifieth, **Thou art a priest for ever after the order of Melchisedec...** By so much was Jesus made a surety of a better testament. And they truly were many priests, because they were not suffered to continue by reason of death: But this man, because he continueth ever, hath an unchangeable priesthood. Wherefore he is able also to save them to the uttermost that come unto God by him, seeing he ever liveth to make intercession for them.

King

(Mic 5:2) But thou, Bethlehem Ephratah, though thou be little among the thousands of Judah, yet out of thee shall

he come forth unto me that is to be ruler in Israel; whose goings forth have been from of old, from everlasting.
(Heb 1:8) But unto the Son he saith, **Thy throne, O God, is for ever and ever: a sceptre of righteousness is the sceptre of thy kingdom.**
(Rev 17:14) These shall make war with the Lamb, and the Lamb shall overcome them: for he is Lord of lords, and <u>King of kings</u>: and they that are with him are called, and chosen, and faithful.
(Phil 2:10) That at the name of Jesus every knee should bow, of things in heaven, and things in earth, and things under the earth; And that every tongue should confess that Jesus Christ is Lord, to the glory of God the Father.
(Rev 1:8,17-18) I am Alpha and Omega, the beginning and the ending, saith the Lord, which is, and which was, and which is to come, the Almighty... And when I saw him, I fell at his feet as dead. And he laid his right hand upon me, saying unto me, Fear not; **I am the first and the last:** I am he that liveth, and was dead; and, behold, I am alive for evermore, Amen; and have the keys of hell and of death.
(John 8:24,58) I said therefore unto you, that ye shall die in your sins: for if ye believe not that **I am** *he*, ye shall die in your sins**...** Jesus

Forgiveness. Based upon the penalty paid at the cross, we believe that the forgiveness of sins is granted by *grace alone* to those who will receive it *by faith alone*.   It must be received as an utterly undeserved gift or it cannot be received at all; because all the credit and glory are *Christ's alone*.

Scriptural references
(Isa 1:18) Come now, and let us reason together, saith the LORD: though your sins be as scarlet, they shall be as

white as snow; though they be red like crimson, they shall be as wool.

(Michah 7:19) He will turn again, he will have compassion upon us; he will subdue our iniquities; and thou wilt cast all their sins into the depths of the sea.

(Eph 2:8-10) For by grace are ye saved through faith; and that not of yourselves: it is the gift of God: Not of works, lest any man should boast. For we are his workmanship, created in Christ Jesus unto good works, which God hath before ordained that we should walk in them.

(Rom 3:20-28) Therefore by the deeds of the law there shall no flesh be justified in his sight: for by the law is the knowledge of sin. But now the righteousness of God without the law is manifested, being witnessed by the law and the prophets; Even the righteousness of God which is <u>by faith of Jesus Christ</u> unto all and upon all them that believe: for there is no difference: For all have sinned, and come short of the glory of God; Being justified freely by his grace through the redemption that is in Christ Jesus: Whom God hath set forth to be a propitiation through faith in his blood, to declare his righteousness for the remission of sins that are past, through the forbearance of God; To declare, I say, at this time his righteousness: that he might be just, and the justifier of him which believeth in Jesus. Where is boasting then? It is excluded. By what law? of works? Nay: but by the law of faith. Therefore we conclude that a man is justified by faith without the deeds of the law.

(Rom 4:3-8) For what saith the scripture? **Abraham believed God, and it was counted unto him for righteousness.** Now to him that worketh is the reward not reckoned of grace, but of debt. But to him that worketh not, but believeth on him that justifieth the ungodly, his faith is counted for righteousness. Even as David also describeth the blessedness of the man, unto whom God imputeth righteousness without works, Saying, **Blessed are they whose iniquities are forgiven, and whose sins are covered. Blessed is the man to whom the Lord will not impute sin.**

(Rom 4:16,22-25) Therefore it is of faith, that it might be by grace; to the end the promise might be sure to all the seed; not to that only which is of the law, but to that also which is of the faith of Abraham; who is the father of us all... And therefore it was imputed to him for righteousness. Now it was not written for his sake alone, that it was imputed to him; But for us also, to whom it shall be imputed, if we believe on him that raised up Jesus our Lord from the dead; who was delivered for our offences, and was raised again for our justification.
(Rom 6:23) For the wages of sin is death; but the gift of God is eternal life through Jesus Christ our Lord.
(Rom 9:30-33) What shall we say then? That the Gentiles, which followed not after righteousness, have attained to righteousness, even the righteousness which is of faith. But Israel, which followed after the law of righteousness, hath not attained to the law of righteousness. Wherefore? Because they sought it not by faith, but as it were by the works of the law. For they stumbled at that stumblingstone; as it is written, **Behold, I lay in Zion a stumblingstone and rock of offence: and whosoever believeth on him shall not be ashamed.**
(Rom 10:9-13) That if thou shalt confess with thy mouth the Lord Jesus, and shalt believe in thine heart that God hath raised him from the dead, thou shalt be saved. For with the heart man believeth unto righteousness; and with the mouth confession is made unto salvation. For the

scripture saith, **Whosoever believeth on him shall not be ashamed.** For there is no difference between the Jew and the Greek: for the same Lord over all is rich unto all that call upon him. **For whosoever shall call upon the name of the Lord shall be saved.**

(Rom 11:6) And if by grace, then is it no more of works: otherwise grace is no more grace. But if it be of works, then is it no more grace: otherwise work is no more work.

(Gal 2:16,21) Knowing that a man is not justified by the works of the law, but by the faith of Jesus Christ, even we have believed in Jesus Christ, that we might be justified by the faith of Christ, and not by the works of the law: for by the works of the law shall no flesh be justified... I do not frustrate the grace of God: for if righteousness come by the law, then Christ is dead in vain.

(Luke 7:47-50) Wherefore I say unto thee, Her sins, which are many, are forgiven; for she loved much: but to whom little is forgiven, the same loveth little. And he said unto her, Thy sins are forgiven. And they that sat at meat with him began to say within themselves, Who is this that forgiveth sins also? And he said to the woman, Thy faith hath saved thee; go in peace.

(Luke 18:10-14) Two men went up into the temple to pray; the one a Pharisee, and the other a publican. The Pharisee stood and prayed thus with himself, God, I thank thee, that I am not as other men are, extortioners, unjust, adulterers, or even as this publican. I fast twice in the week, I give tithes of all that I possess. And the publican, standing afar off, would not lift up so much as his eyes unto heaven, but smote upon his breast, saying, God be merciful to me a sinner. I tell you, this man went down to his house justified rather than the other: for every one that exalteth himself shall be abased; and he that humbleth himself shall be exalted.

(John 3:16-18) For God so loved the world, that he gave his only begotten Son, that whosoever believeth in him should not perish, but have everlasting life. For God sent not his Son into the world to condemn the world; but that the world through him might be saved. He that believeth on him is not condemned: but he that believeth not is condemned already, because he hath not believed in the name of the only begotten Son of God.
(John 6:47) Verily, verily, I say unto you, He that believeth on me hath everlasting life.
(Acts 16:31) And they said, Believe on the Lord Jesus Christ, and thou shalt be saved, and thy house.

(Titus 3:5-7) Not by works of righteousness which we have done, but according to his mercy he saved us, by the washing of regeneration, and renewing of the Holy Ghost; which he shed on us abundantly through Jesus Christ our Saviour; That being justified by his grace, we should be made heirs according to the hope of eternal life.
(Heb 10:14-17) For by one offering he hath perfected for ever them that are sanctified. Whereof the Holy Ghost also is a witness to us: for after that he had said before, **This is the covenant that I will make with them after those days, saith the Lord, I will put my laws into their hearts, and in their minds will I write them; And their sins and iniquities will I remember no more.**
(Heb 11:6) But without faith it is impossible to please him: for he that cometh to God must believe that he is, and that he is a rewarder of them that diligently seek him.
(1John 5:11-13) And this is the record, that God hath given to us eternal life, and this life is in his Son. He that hath the Son hath life; and he that hath not the Son of God hath

not life. These things have I written unto you that believe on the name of the Son of God; tha

Repentance. We *turn* (repent) from self-reliance for our salvation, to trusting alone in the completed work of Jesus upon the cross to purchase the perfect pardon of all our sin, forever.

Scriptural References:
(Mark 1:15) And saying, The time is fulfilled, and the kingdom of God is at hand: repent ye, and believe the gospel.
(Mark 10:28-30) Then Peter began to say unto him, Lo, we have left all, and have followed thee. And Jesus answered and said, Verily I say unto you, There is no man that hath left house, or brethren, or sisters, or father, or mother, or wife, or children, or lands, for my sake, and the gospel's, but he shall receive an hundredfold now in this time, houses, and brethren, and sisters, and mothers, and children, and lands, with persecutions; and in the world to come eternal life.
(Luke 3:3) And he came into all the country about Jordan, preaching the baptism of repentance for the remission of sins;
(Matt 6:33) But seek ye first the kingdom of God, and his righteousness; and all these things shall be added unto you.

(Acts 3:19) Repent ye therefore, and be converted, that your sins may be blotted out, when the times of refreshing shall come from the presence of the Lord
(Acts 11:18) When they heard these things, they held their peace, and glorified God, saying, Then hath God also to the Gentiles granted repentance unto life.

(Luke 18:9-14) And he spake this parable unto certain which <u>trusted in themselves that they were righteous</u>, and despised others: Two men went up into the temple to pray; the one a Pharisee, and the other a publican. The Pharisee stood and prayed thus with himself, God, I thank thee, that I am not as other men are, extortioners, unjust, adulterers, or even as this publican. I fast twice in the week, I give tithes of all that I possess. And the publican, standing afar off, would not lift up so much as his eyes unto heaven, but smote upon his breast, saying, God be merciful to me a sinner. I tell you, this man went down to his house justified rather than the other: for every one that exalteth himself shall be abased; and he that humbleth himself shall be exalted.

(Acts 20:21) Testifying both to the Jews, and also to the Greeks, repentance toward God, and faith toward our Lord Jesus Christ.

(Luke 24:46-47) And said unto them, Thus it is written, and thus it behoved Christ to suffer, and to rise from the dead the third day: And that repentance and remission of sins should be preached in his name among all nations, beginning at Jerusalem.

(John 7:37) In the last day, that great day of the feast, Jesus stood and cried, saying, If any man thirst, let him come unto me, and drink.

(Acts 16:31) And they said, Believe on the Lord Jesus Christ, and thou shalt be saved, and thy house.

(Rom 10:9-13) That if thou shalt confess with thy mouth the Lord Jesus, and shalt believe in thine heart that God hath raised him from the dead, thou shalt be saved. For with the heart man believeth unto righteousness; and with the mouth confession is made unto salvation. For the scripture saith, **Whosoever believeth on him shall not be ashamed.** For there is no difference between the Jew and

the Greek: for the same Lord over all is rich unto all that call upon him. **For whosoever shall call upon the name of the Lord shall be saved.**
(Jas 4:6) But he giveth more grace. Wherefore he saith, **God resisteth the proud, but giveth grace unto the humble.**

(Deut 30:19) I call heaven and earth to record this day against you, that I have set before you life and death, blessing and cursing: therefore choose life, that both thou and thy seed may live:
(Josh 24:15) And if it seem evil unto you to serve the LORD, choose you this day whom ye will serve; whether the gods which your fathers served that were on the other side of the flood, or the gods of the Amorites, in whose land ye dwell: but as for me and my house, we will serve the LORD.
(2Chr 7:14) If my people, which are called by my name, shall humble themselves, and pray, and seek my face, and turn from their wicked ways; then will I hear from heaven, and will forgive their sin, and will heal their land.

(Prov 1:28-29) Then shall they call upon me, but I will not answer; they shall seek me early, but they shall not find me: For that they hated knowledge, and did not choose the fear of the LORD
(Prov 3:5) Trust in the LORD with all thine heart; and lean not unto thine own understanding.
(Jer 17:5) Thus saith the LORD; Cursed be the man that trusteth in man, and maketh flesh his arm, and whose heart departeth from the LORD.
Repentance defined: to turn from, change direction in thinking.
Examples...

(Gen 6:6) And it <u>repented</u> the LORD that he had made man on the earth, and it grieved him at his heart.
(Exod 32:14) And the LORD <u>repented</u> of the evil [*judgment*] which he thought to do unto his people.
(Ps 135:14) For the LORD will judge his people, and he will <u>repent</u> himself concerning his servants.
(Jer 18:10) If it do evil in my sight, that it obey not my voice, then I will <u>repent</u> of the good, wherewith I said I would benefit them.
(Ezek 14:6) Therefore say unto the house of Israel, Thus saith the Lord GOD; <u>Repent</u>, and <u>turn</u> yourselves from your idols; and turn away your faces from all your abominations.
(Jonah 3:9) Who can tell if God will turn and <u>repent</u>, and <u>turn</u> away from his fierce anger, that we perish not?

Works. We believe in doing good works in grateful *response* to our pardon, not to cause it. From our faith, acts of response will flow such as: obedience, compassion, baptism, communion, prayer, etc.

Scriptural References
(Matt 7:16-20) Ye shall know them by their fruits. Do men gather grapes of thorns, or figs of thistles? Even so every good tree bringeth forth good fruit; but a corrupt tree bringeth forth evil fruit. A good tree cannot bring forth evil fruit, neither can a corrupt tree bring forth good fruit. Every tree that bringeth not forth good fruit is hewn down, and cast into the fire. Wherefore by their fruits ye shall know them.

(John 15:4-5) Abide in me, and I in you. As the branch cannot bear fruit of itself, except it abide in the vine; no more can ye, except ye abide in me. I am the vine, ye are the branches: He that abideth in me, and I in him, the same bringeth forth much fruit: for without me ye can do nothing.

(John 15:12) This is my commandment, That ye love one another, as I have loved you.

(Acts 16:31-33) And they said, Believe on the Lord Jesus Christ, and thou shalt be saved, and thy house. And they spake unto him the word of the Lord, and to all that were in his house. And he took them the same hour of the night, and washed their stripes; and was baptized, he and all his, straightway.

(1Cor 11:23-26) For I have received of the Lord that which also I delivered unto you, That the Lord Jesus the same night in which he was betrayed took bread: And when he had given thanks, he brake it, and said, Take, eat: this is my body, which is broken for you: this do in remembrance of me. After the same manner also he took the cup, when he had supped, saying, This cup is the new testament in my blood: this do ye, as oft as ye drink it, in remembrance of me. For as often as ye eat this bread, and drink this cup, ye do shew the Lord's death till he come.

(Eph 2:8-10) For by grace are ye saved through faith; and that not of yourselves: it is the gift of God: not of works, lest any man should boast. For we are his workmanship, created in Christ Jesus unto good works, which God hath before ordained that we should walk in them.

(Gal 2:16) Knowing that a man is not justified by the works of the law, but by the faith of Jesus Christ, even we have believed in Jesus Christ, that we might be justified by the faith of Christ, and not by the works of the law: for by the works of the law shall no flesh be justified.

(Gal 5:22-25) But the fruit of the Spirit is love, joy, peace, longsuffering, gentleness, goodness, faith, meekness, temperance: against such there is no law. And they that are Christ's have crucified the flesh with the affections and lusts. If we live in the Spirit, let us also walk in the Spirit. (Rom 11:6) And if by grace, then is it no more of works: otherwise grace is no more grace. But if it be of works, then is it no more grace: otherwise work is no more work. **(Rom 1:5)** By whom we have received grace and apostleship, for obedience to the faith among all nations, for his name

(Rom 12:1-2) I beseech you therefore, brethren, by the mercies of God, that ye present your bodies a living sacrifice, holy, acceptable unto God, which is your reasonable service. And be not conformed to this world: but be ye transformed by the renewing of your mind, that ye may prove what is that good, and acceptable, and perfect, will of God.

(Rom 14:23) ...for whatsoever is not of faith is sin.

(Col 1:5-6) For the hope which is laid up for you in heaven, whereof ye heard before in the word of the truth of the gospel; which is come unto you, as it is in all the world; and bringeth forth fruit, as it doth also in you, since the day ye heard of it, and knew the grace of God in truth

(Titus 3:5) Not by works of righteousness which we have done, but according to his mercy he saved us, by the washing of regeneration, and renewing of the Holy Ghost

(Titus 2:11-12) For the grace of God that bringeth salvation hath appeared to all men, teaching us that, denying ungodliness and worldly lusts, we should live soberly, righteously, and godly, in this present world

(Heb 9:14) How much more shall the blood of Christ, who through the eternal Spirit offered himself without spot to

God, purge your conscience from dead works to serve the living God?

(Heb 12:1-2) Wherefore seeing we also are compassed about with so great a cloud of witnesses, let us lay aside every weight, and the sin which doth so easily beset us, and let us run with patience the race that is set before us, Looking unto Jesus the author and finisher of our faith; who for the joy that was set before him endured the cross, despising the shame, and is set down at the right hand of the throne of God.

(Heb 13:15) By him therefore let us offer the sacrifice of praise to God continually, that is, the fruit of our lips giving thanks to his name.

(Jas 2:20-26) But wilt thou know, O vain man, that faith without works is dead? Was not Abraham our father justified by works, when he had offered Isaac his son upon the altar [Gen 22:10]? Seest thou how faith wrought with his works, and by works was faith made perfect? And the scripture was fulfilled which saith, **Abraham believed God, and it was imputed unto him for righteousness** [Gen 15:6]: and he was called the Friend of God. Ye see then how that by works a man is justified, and not by faith only. Likewise also was not Rahab the harlot justified by works, when she had received the messengers, and had sent them out another way? For as the body without the spirit is dead, so faith without works is dead also.

(Jas 3:18) And the fruit of righteousness is sown in peace of them that make peace.

(1John 4:19) We love him, because he first loved us.

Inheritance. As believers, we are Christ's true church, and have consequently received many other spiritual blessings, including: reconciliation and friendship with a Holy God, the indwelling of the Holy Spirit, adoption as children of God into His family, and *eternal life* now and in His kingdom.

Scriptural references

(John 1:12-13) But as many as received him, to them gave he power to become the sons of God, even to them that believe on his name: Which were born, not of blood, nor of the will of the flesh, nor of the will of man, but of God.

(John 3:16) For God so loved the world, that he gave his only begotten Son, that whosoever believeth in him should not perish, but have everlasting life.

(John 5:24) Verily, verily, I say unto you, He that heareth my word, and believeth on him that sent me, hath everlasting life, and shall not come into condemnation; but is passed from death unto life.

(John 6:47) Verily, verily, I say unto you, He that believeth on me hath everlasting life.

(John 10:27-28) My sheep hear my voice, and I know them, and they follow me: And I give unto them eternal life; and they shall never perish, neither shall any man pluck them out of my hand.

(John 14:16-18) And I will pray the Father, and he shall give you another Comforter, that he may abide with you for ever; even the Spirit of truth; whom the world cannot receive, because it seeth him not, neither knoweth him: but ye know him; for he dwelleth with you, and shall be in you. I will not leave you comfortless: I will come to you. (John 15:26) But when the Comforter is come, whom I will send unto you from the Father, even the Spirit of truth, which proceedeth from the Father, he shall testify of me (John 16:13-14) Howbeit when he, the Spirit of truth, is come, he will guide you into all truth: for he shall not speak of himself; but whatsoever he shall hear, that shall he speak: and he will shew you things to come. He shall glorify me: for he shall receive of mine, and shall shew it unto you.

(Rom 5:1-2) Therefore being justified by faith, we have peace with God through our Lord Jesus Christ: by whom also we have access by faith into this grace wherein we stand, and rejoice in hope of the glory of God.

(Rom 8: 9,15-18,23-30) But ye are not in the flesh, but in the Spirit, if so be that the Spirit of God dwell in you. Now if any man have not the Spirit of Christ, he is none of his... For ye have not received the spirit of bondage again to fear; but ye have received the Spirit of adoption, whereby we cry, Abba, Father. The Spirit itself beareth witness with our spirit, that we are the children of God and if children, then heirs; heirs of God, and joint-heirs with Christ; if so be that we suffer with him, that we may be also glorified together. For I reckon that the sufferings of this present time are not worthy to be compared with the glory which shall be revealed in us... And not only they, but ourselves also, which have the firstfruits of the Spirit, even we ourselves groan within ourselves, waiting for the adoption, to wit, the redemption of our body. For we are saved by hope: but hope that is seen is not hope: for what a man seeth, why doth he yet hope for? But if we hope for that we see not, then do we with patience wait for it. Likewise the Spirit also helpeth our infirmities: for we know not what we should pray for as we ought: but the Spirit itself maketh intercession for us with groanings which cannot be uttered. And he that searcheth the hearts knoweth what is the mind of the Spirit, because he maketh intercession for the saints according to the will of God. And we know that all things work together for good to them that love

God, to them who are the called according to his purpose. For whom he did foreknow, he also did predestinate to be conformed to the image of his Son, that he might be the firstborn among many brethren. Moreover whom he did predestinate, them he also called: and whom he called, them he also justified: and whom he justified, them he also glorified.

(1Cor 2:12) Now we have not received the spirit of the world, but the Spirit who is from God, so that we may know the things that are freely given to us by God.

(1Cor 15:42,53-55) So also is the resurrection of the dead. It is sown in corruption; it is raised in incorruption... For this corruptible must put on incorruption, and this mortal must put on immortality. So when this corruptible shall have put on incorruption, and this mortal shall have put on immortality, then shall be brought to pass the saying that is written, **Death is swallowed up in victory. O death, where is thy sting? O grave, where is thy victory?**

(2Cor 5:17-19) Therefore if any man be in Christ, he is a new creature: old things are passed away; behold, all things are become new. And all things are of God, who hath reconciled us to himself by Jesus Christ, and hath given to us the ministry of reconciliation; to wit, that God was in Christ, reconciling the world unto himself, not imputing their trespasses unto them; and hath committed unto us the word of reconciliation.

(Gal 3:18,29) For if the inheritance be of the law, it is no more of promise: but God gave it to Abraham by promise... And if ye be Christ's, then are ye Abraham's seed, and heirs according to the promise.

(1Thess 4:15-18) For this we say unto you by the word of the Lord, that we which are alive and remain unto the coming of the Lord shall not prevent them which are asleep. For the Lord himself shall descend from heaven with a shout, with the voice of the archangel, and with the trump of God: and the dead in Christ shall rise first: Then we which are alive and remain shall be caught up together with them in the clouds, to meet the Lord in the air: and so shall we ever be with the Lord. Wherefore comfort one another with these words.

(Titus 3:5-7) Not by works of righteousness which we have done, but according to his mercy he saved us, by the washing of regeneration, and renewing of the Holy Ghost; which he shed on us abundantly through Jesus Christ our Saviour; that being justified by his grace, we should be made heirs according to the hope of eternal life.

(1John 2:25) And this is the promise that he hath promised us, even eternal life.

(Rev 7:9-12) After this I beheld, and, lo, a great multitude, which no man could number, of all nations, and kindreds, and people, and tongues, stood before the throne, and before the Lamb, clothed with white robes, and palms in their hands; And cried with a loud voice, saying, Salvation to our God which sitteth upon the throne, and unto the Lamb. And all the angels stood round about the throne, and about the elders and the four beasts, and fell before the throne on their faces, and worshipped God, saying, Amen: Blessing, and glory, and wisdom, and thanksgiving, and honour, and power, and might, be

10. **Deception**. We also acknowledge the existence of the great counterfeiter of prophecy, miracles, emotions, and feelings: Satan. Therefore, we take seriously God's command to test all these things *according to scripture*.

Scriptural References:

(Deut 11:16) Take heed to yourselves, that your heart be not deceived, and ye turn aside, and serve other gods, and worship them;

(Deut 13:1-5) If there arise among you a prophet, or a dreamer of dreams, and giveth thee a sign or a wonder, and the sign or the wonder come to pass, whereof he spake unto thee, saying, Let us go after other gods, which thou hast not known, and let us serve them; Thou shalt not hearken unto the words of that prophet, or that dreamer of dreams: for the LORD your God proveth you, to know whether ye love the LORD your God with all your heart and with all your soul. Ye shall walk after the LORD your God, and fear him, and keep his commandments, and obey his voice, and ye shall serve him, and cleave unto him. And that prophet, or that dreamer of dreams, shall be put to death; because he hath spoken to turn you away from the LORD your God...
(Deut 18:20-22) But the prophet, which shall presume to speak a word in my name, which I have not commanded him to speak, or that shall speak in the name of other gods, even that prophet shall die. And if thou say in thine heart, How shall we know the word which the LORD hath not spoken? When a prophet speaketh in the name of the LORD, if the thing follow not, nor come to pass, that is the thing which the LORD hath not spoken, but the prophet hath spoken it presumptuously: thou shalt not be afraid of him.
(Isa 44:20) He feedeth on ashes: a deceived heart hath turned him aside, that he cannot deliver his soul, nor say, Is there not a lie in my right hand?

(Jer 17:9) The heart is deceitful above all things, and desperately wicked: who can know it?

(Ezek 22:28) And her prophets have daubed them with untempered morter, seeing vanity, and divining lies unto them, saying, Thus saith the Lord GOD, when the LORD hath not spoken.

(Matt 7:15) Beware of false prophets, which come to you in sheep's clothing, but inwardly they are ravening wolves. **(John 7:24)** Judge not according to the appearance, but judge righteous judgment.

(Matt 15:19) For out of the heart proceed evil thoughts, murders, adulteries, fornications, thefts, false witness, blasphemies

(Matt 24:11,23-26) And many false prophets shall rise, and shall deceive many... Then if any man shall say unto you, Lo, here is Christ, or there; believe it not. For there shall arise false Christs, and false prophets, and shall shew great signs and wonders; insomuch that, if it were possible, they shall deceive the very elect. Behold, I have told you before. Wherefore if they shall say unto you, Behold, he is in the desert; go not forth: behold, he is in the secret chambers; believe it not.
(Mark 14:56) For many bare false witness against him, but their witness agreed not together.
(Mark 4:15) And these are they by the way side, where the word is sown; but when they have heard, Satan cometh immediately, and <u>taketh away the word</u> that was sown in their hearts.

(Luke 22:31) And the Lord said, Simon, Simon, behold, Satan hath desired to have you, that he may sift you as wheat

(John 8:44) Ye are of your father the devil, and the lusts of your father ye will do. He was a murderer from the beginning, and abode not in the truth, because there is no truth in him. When he speaketh a lie, he speaketh of his own: for he is a liar, and the father of it.

(Acts 17:11) These were more noble than those in Thessalonica, in that they received the word with all readiness of mind, and searched the scriptures daily, whether those things were so.
(Eph 6:11-17) Put on the whole armour of God, that ye may be able to stand against the wiles of the devil. For we wrestle not against flesh and blood, but against principalities, against powers, against the rulers of the darkness of this world, against spiritual wickedness in high places. Wherefore take unto you the whole armour of God, that ye may be able to withstand in the evil day, and having done all, to stand. Stand therefore, having your loins girt about with truth, and having on the breastplate of righteousness; and your feet shod with the preparation of the gospel of peace; Above all, taking the shield of faith, wherewith ye shall be able to quench all the fiery darts of the wicked. And take the helmet of salvation, and the sword of the Spirit, which is the word of God:

(1Thess 5:21) Prove all things; hold fast that which is good. (2Cor 11:2-4,13-15) For I am jealous over you with godly jealousy: for I have espoused you to one husband, that I may present you as a chaste virgin to Christ. But I fear, lest by any means, as the serpent beguiled Eve through his subtilty, so your minds should be corrupted from the simplicity that is in Christ. For if he that cometh preacheth another Jesus, whom we have not preached, or if ye receive another spirit, which ye have not received, or another gospel, which ye have not accepted, ye might well bear with him... For such are false apostles, deceitful workers, transforming themselves into the apostles of Christ. And no marvel; for Satan himself is transformed into an angel of light. Therefore it is no great thing if his ministers also be transformed as the ministers of righteousness; whose end shall be according to their works.

(Gal 2:4) Now this matter arose because of the false brothers with false pretenses who slipped in unnoticed to spy on our freedom that we have in Christ Jesus, to make us slaves.

(2Thess 2:9-12,15) The arrival of the lawless one will be by Satan's working with all kinds of miracles and signs and false wonders, and with every kind of evil deception directed against those who are perishing, because they found no place in their hearts for the truth so as to be saved. Consequently God sends on them a deluding influence so that they will believe what is false. And so all of them who have not believed the truth but have delighted in evil will be condemned... Therefore, brethren, stand fast, and hold the traditions which ye have been taught, whether by word, or our epistle.

(2Tim 2:15) Study to shew thyself approved unto God, a workman that needeth not to be ashamed, rightly dividing the word of truth.

(2Tim 3:14-17) But continue thou in the things which thou hast learned and hast been assured of, knowing of whom thou hast learned them; and that from a child thou hast known the holy scriptures, which are able to make thee wise unto salvation through faith which is in Christ

Jesus. All scripture is given by inspiration of God, and is profitable for doctrine, for reproof, for correction, for instruction in righteousness: That the man of God may be perfect, throughly furnished unto all good works.
(2Tim 4:2-4) Preach the word; be instant in season, out of season; reprove, rebuke, exhort with all longsuffering and doctrine. For the time will come when they will not endure sound doctrine; but after their own lusts shall they heap to themselves teachers, having itching ears; and they shall turn away their ears from the truth, and shall be turned unto fables.
(1Pet 5:8) Be sober, be vigilant; because your adversary the devil, as a roaring lion, walketh about, seeking whom he may devour
(2Pet 2:1-3) But false prophets arose among the people, just as there will be false teachers among you. These false teachers will infiltrate your midst with destructive heresies, even to the point of denying the Master who bought them. As a result, they will bring swift destruction on themselves. And many will follow their debauched lifestyles. Because of these false teachers, the way of truth will be slandered. And in their greed they will exploit you with deceptive words. Their condemnation pronounced long ago is not sitting idly by; their destruction is not asleep.

(1John 4:1) Dear friends, do not believe every spirit, but test the spirits to determine if they are from God, because many false prophets have gone out into the world.
(Rev 2:2) 'I know your works as well as your labor and steadfast endurance, and that you cannot tolerate evil. You have even put to the test those who refer to themselves as apostles (but are not), and have discovered that they are false.

(Rev 16:14) For they are the spirits of devils, working miracles..

Conclusion and Prayer

A shift has been occurring in some conservative evangelical circles in a more Pentecostal direction. They "have adopted certain Pentecostal practices such as **healing the sick, casting out demons, and receiving prophetic revelations.**" Some believe that the so-called 'baptism in the Holy Spirit' happens at conversion...and that tongues is simply one of many spiritual gifts and not the only evidence of a particular spiritual experience." Such conservative evangelicals, therefore, do not view themselves as Pentecostals or charismatics.

Our Christian experience rises and falls with the revelation we decide to accept or reject. The truth cannot be buried, it will rise to speak for itself. Everything about God is received by spiritual revelation. If we have experienced it, let us pray for our brothers and sisters that haven't yet and if they reject it, it does not stop them from going to be with the Lord or be effective in His hands.

Father, thank You for the many faces and dimensions of You that You decide to unfold to us individually and collectively. Help us to carry our brothers and sisters along, praying, just like Elisha prayed in 2 Kings 6:17 for them to see and receive the revelation we have received and experienced. So they can see what we see and benefit Your kingdom thereby in Jesus name, amen

Shalom!

Chapter 20 - The Christian Church – Civil Wars In The Churches – A Spiritual Warfare Strategy, A Divine Revelation By Rick Joyner And Why We Must Pay Attention – The Final Quest

Introduction

We are looking at civil wars in the churches necessitated by disunity, an end time spiritual warfare strategy by the accuser of the brethren as a final onslaught on the church of Jesus Christ revealed by God to Rick Joyner and why we must pay very, very careful attention with corresponding corrective action before it is too late. Here it is...

Key verses

1 Corinthians 1:12,13 New Living Translation

[12] Some of you are saying, "I am a follower of Paul"; and others say that they are for Apollos or for Peter; and some that they alone are the true followers of Christ. [13] **And so, in effect, you have broken Christ into many pieces.**
But did I, Paul, die for your sins? Were any of you baptized in my name?

John 17:21 English Standard Version (ESV)

²¹ that they may all be one, just as you, Father, are in me, and I in you, that they also may be in us, so that the world may believe that you have sent me.

Psalm 133:1,2
Behold, how good and how pleasant it is For brethren to dwell together in unity! 2It is like the precious oil upon the head, Coming down upon the beard, Even Aaron's beard, Coming down upon the edge of his robes....

Matthew 12:22-28 New King James Version (NKJV)
A House Divided Cannot Stand
²² Then one was brought to Him who was demon-possessed, blind and mute; and He healed him, so that the [a]blind and mute man both spoke and saw. ²³ And all the multitudes were amazed and said, "Could this be the Son of David?"
²⁴ Now when the Pharisees heard *it* they said, "This *fellow* does not cast out demons except by [b]Beelzebub, the ruler of the demons."
²⁵ But Jesus knew their thoughts, and said to them: **"Every kingdom divided against itself is brought to desolation, and every city or house divided against itself will not stand.** ²⁶ If Satan casts out Satan, he is divided against himself. How then will his kingdom stand? ²⁷ And if I cast out demons by Beelzebub, by whom do your sons cast *them* out? Therefore they shall be your judges. ²⁸ But if I cast out demons by the Spirit of God, surely the kingdom of God has come upon you.

The Evil Army Unleashed On The Church As Seen By Rick Joyner

I saw a demonic army so large that it stretched as far as I could see. It was separated into divisions, with each carrying a different banner. The foremost and most powerful divisions were Pride, Self-righteousness, Respectability, Selfish Ambition, and Unrighteous Judgment, but the largest of all was Jealousy. The leader of this vast army was the Accuser of the Brethren himself. I knew that there were many more evil divisions beyond my scope of vision, but these were the vanguard of this terrible horde from hell that was now being released against the church.

The weapons carried by this horde had names on them: the swords were named Intimidation; the spears were named Treachery; and their arrows were named Accusations, Gossip, Slander and Faultfinding. Scouts and smaller companies of demons with such names as Rejection, Bitterness, Impatience, Un-forgiveness and Lust were sent in advance of this army to prepare for the main attack. I knew in my heart that the church had never faced anything like this before.

The main assignment of this army was to cause division. It was sent to attack every level of relationship-churches with each other, congregations with their pastors, husbands and wives, children and parents, and even children with each other. The scouts were sent to locate the openings in churches, families or individuals that rejection, bitterness, lust, etc., could exploit and make a larger breech for the divisions that were coming.

The most shocking part of this vision was that this horde was not riding on horses, but on Christians! Most of them were well-dressed, respectable, and had the appearance

of being refined and educated. These were Christians who had opened themselves to the powers of darkness to such a degree that the enemy could use them and they would think that they were being used by God. The Accuser knows that a house divided cannot stand, and this army represented his ultimate attempt to bring such complete division to the church that she would completely fall from grace.

The Christian Prisoners As Seen By The Vision Of Rick Joyner

Trailing behind these first divisions was a vast multitude of other Christians who were prisoners of this army. They were all wounded, and were guarded by little demons of Fear. There seemed to be more prisoners than there were demons in the army. Surprisingly, these prisoners still had their swords and shields, but they did not use them. It was shocking to see that so many could be kept captive by so few of these little demons of Fear. These could have easily been destroyed or driven off if the prisoners had just used their weapons.

Above the prisoners the sky was black with vultures named Depression. These would land on the shoulders of a prisoner and vomit on him. The vomit was Condemnation. When the vomit hit a prisoner he would stand up and march a little straighter for a while, and then slump over, even weaker than before. Again, I wondered why the prisoners did not simply kill these vultures with their swords, which they could have easily done.

Occasionally a weak prisoner would stumble and fall. As soon as he or she hit the ground, the other prisoners would begin stabbing them with their swords, scorning them as they did so. They would then call for the vultures to begin devouring the fallen one even before they were dead.

As I watched, I realized that these prisoners thought that the vomit of condemnation was truth from God. Then I understood that these prisoners actually thought they were marching in the army of God! This is why they did not kill the little demons of fear, or the vultures-they thought these were messengers from God! The darkness from the cloud of vultures made it so hard for these prisoners to see that they naively accepted everything that happened to them as being from the Lord.

The only food provided for these prisoners was the vomit from the vultures. Those who refused to eat it simple weakened until they fell. Those who did eat it were strengthened, but with the strength of the evil one. They would then begin to vomit on the others. When one began to do this a demon that was waiting for a ride would be given this one and he or she would be promoted to the front divisions.
Even worse than the vomit from the vultures was a repulsive slime that these demons were urinating and defecating upon the Christians they rode.

This slime was the pride, selfish ambition, etc., that was the nature of the division they were a part of. However, this slime made the Christians feel so much better than the condemnation that they easily believed that the demons were messengers of God, and they actually thought this slime was the anointing of the Holy Spirit.

What Was God's Response To Rick Joyner From The First Episode?

Then the voice of the Lord came to me saying, "This is the beginning of the enemy's last day army. This is Satan's ultimate deception, and his ultimate power of destruction is released when he uses Christians to attack other Christians. Throughout the ages he has used this army, but never has he been able to capture so many to be used for his evil purposes. Do not fear. I have an army too. You must now stand and fight, because there is no longer any place to hide from this war. You must fight for My Kingdom, for truth, and for those who have been deceived."

I had been so repulsed and outraged by the evil army that I had wanted to die rather than live in such a world. However, this word from the Lord was so encouraging that I immediately began yelling to the Christian prisoners that they were being deceived, thinking that they would listen to me. When I did this, it seemed that the whole army turned to look at me, but I kept yelling. I thought that the Christians were going to wake up and realize what was happening to them, but instead many of them started reaching for their arrows to shoot at me. The others just hesitated as if they did not know what to make of me. I knew then that I had done this prematurely, and that it had been a very foolish mistake.

Conclusion and Prayer

The battle we face in this end times as body of the Lord Jesus Christ is more from within than from without. If we win the battle within us, no external power can do us harm. They will try but they cannot succeed. A kingdom divided against itself cannot stand – either demonic or God's kingdom. The matter of disunity has become a cancer in the body of Christ. I pray and hope that this vision by Rick Joyner in the final Quest will become a wakeup call.

Dear Lord God, wake us up to the need to address the seeming distance between us Your body of believers necessitate by difference in how we see You and relate with You. Help us to set aside our preconception, revelations and everything else that points to disunity in Your body and as we do this , grant us grace to engage in love with our brethren from the other divide in Jesus name, Amen

Shalom!

Chapter 21 - The Christian Church – If God's House Is a House of Prayer For All People, What then should be the Kind of Prayer He would love to Answer?

Introduction

We are looking at this simple question –Since Gods house is a house of prayer, what then should be the kind of prayer we need to prayer for God to answer our prayers? Why are so much prayer going up to heaven from Gods house and seems to be falling on deaf ears? Why are prayers falling back on our heads unanswered?
We desire success in our pursuit of God but God is saying success starts with a string of right choices as He prompts us to make a choice at every point we engage with Him.

NUGGETS OF WISDOM

How do i determine **SPIRITUAL MATURITY** in my own life? Spiritual Maturity is always determined by my **WILLINGNESS** to **SACRIFICE** my own **DESIRES** for the interest of the **KINGDOM** and or for the sake of **OTHERS** ..look up these verses: **Matthew 22:37; John 5:19,30 and Mark 10:21**

Key verses

Isaiah 56:7 New American Standard Bible (NASB)

7 Even those I will bring to My holy mountain
And make them joyful in **My house of prayer**.
Their burnt offerings and their sacrifices will be acceptable
on My altar;
For **My house will be called a house of prayer for all the
peoples."**

Jeremiah 7:11 New American Standard Bible (NASB)
11 Has this house, which is called by My name, become a
den of robbers in your sight? Behold, I, even I, have seen
it," declares the Lord.

Matthew 21:13 New American Standard Bible (NASB)
13 And He *said to them, "It is written, 'My house shall be
called a house of prayer'; but you are making it a robbers'
[a]den."

Luke 11:1-4 Amplified Bible (AMP)
Instruction about Prayer
11 It happened that while Jesus was praying in a certain
place, after He finished, one of His disciples said to Him,
"Lord, teach us to pray just as John also taught his
disciples." 2 He said to them,
"When you pray, say:
'[b]Father, hallowed be Your name.
[d]Your kingdom come.
3
'Give us each day our [e]daily bread.
4
'And forgive us our sins,
For we ourselves also forgive everyone who is indebted to
us [who has offended or wronged us].
And [f]lead us not into temptation [[g]but rescue us from
evil].'"

Matthew 7:7 Living Bible (TLB)

7 "Ask, and you will be given what you ask for. Seek, and you will find. Knock, and the door will be opened.

Matthew 6:32-33 Living Bible (TLB)

31-32 "So don't worry at all about having enough food and clothing. Why be like the heathen? For they take pride in all these things and are deeply concerned about them. But your heavenly Father already knows perfectly well that you need them, **33 and he will give them to you if you give him first place in your life and live as he wants you to.**

Lamentations 3:22-25 Living Bible (TLB)

22 *his compassion never ends.* It is only the Lord's mercies that have kept us from complete destruction. 23 Great is his faithfulness; his loving-kindness begins afresh each day. 24 My soul claims the Lord as my inheritance; therefore I will hope in him. 25 The Lord is wonderfully good to those who wait for him, to those who seek for him.

John 5:1-16 Living Bible (TLB)

5 Afterwards Jesus returned to Jerusalem for one of the Jewish religious holidays. 2 Inside the city, near the Sheep Gate, was Bethesda Pool, with five covered platforms or porches surrounding it. 3 Crowds of sick folks—lame, blind, or with paralyzed limbs—lay on the platforms (waiting for a certain movement of the water, 4 for an angel of the Lord came from time to time and disturbed the water, and the first person to step down into it afterwards was healed).[a]

5 One of the men lying there had been sick for thirty-eight years. **6 When Jesus saw him and knew how long he had been ill, he asked him, "Would you like to get well?"**
7 "I can't," the sick man said, "for I have no one to help me into the pool at the movement of the water. While I am trying to get there, someone else always gets in ahead of me."
8 Jesus told him, "Stand up, roll up your sleeping mat and go on home!"
9 Instantly, the man was healed! He rolled up the mat and began walking!
But it was on the Sabbath when this miracle was done.
10 So the Jewish leaders objected. They said to the man who was cured, "You can't work on the Sabbath! It's illegal to carry that sleeping mat!"
11 "The man who healed me told me to," was his reply.
12 "Who said such a thing as that?" they demanded.
13 The man didn't know, and Jesus had disappeared into the crowd. **14 But afterwards Jesus found him in the Temple and told him, "Now you are well; don't sin as you did before,[b] or something even worse may happen to you."**
15 Then the man went to find the Jewish leaders and told them it was Jesus who had healed him.
16 So they began harassing Jesus as a Sabbath breaker.

1 Corinthians 1:12,13 New Living Translation

12 Some of you are saying, "I am a follower of Paul"; and others say that they are for Apollos or for Peter; and some that they alone are the true followers of Christ. **13 And so, in effect, you have broken Christ into many pieces.**

But did I, Paul, die for your sins? Were any of you baptized in my name?

John 17:21 English Standard Version (ESV)
21 that they may all be one, just as you, Father, are in me, and I in you, that they also may be in us, so that the world may believe that you have sent me.

Psalm 133:1,2
Behold, how good and how pleasant it is For brethren to dwell together in unity! 2It is like the precious oil upon the head, Coming down upon the beard, Even Aaron's beard, Coming down upon the edge of his robes....

Matthew 12:25 New King James Version (NKJV)
A House Divided Cannot Stand
25 But Jesus knew their thoughts, and said to them: **"Every kingdom divided against itself is brought to desolation, and every city or house divided against itself will not stand.**

Five Points to help clear the air

Let's take a look at five (5) points that could help us narrow down and clear the air in our prayer closet so that the Lord will bring illumination to our spirit man so we can make a successful choice today when we go to the foot of the cross to present our petitions before Him.

1. I must be ready to say YES no matter the outcome

I tell people, when we engage God over an issue over a period of time, have we cared to listen to what He has to say if He is prompting us to take a step, are we willing to say YES, not my way but Yours? Are we willing to drop our desires for His own desires? Are we dead to self and alive to Him? Make a YES decision today before, during and after prayer with our heavenly father and watch out for the outcome

2. Advancement of His Will and His Kingdom

Can we line up our needs in the light of His Kingdom and His will? Is what I am asking for in line with the advancement of His will and His Kingdom? Or is this for my kingdom? His will and His kingdom comes first. Why don't we start by asking Him to filter what we asking for and cause it to line up with what brings Him pleasure

3. Sin in the camp

There is what we call deliberate and willful sin. Are we living in rebellion to Gods instruction? Have we pitched tent with darkness? Light and darkness cannot mingle. One has to go for the other to emerge. There is no sitting on the fence in God. It is either black or white. Am I at peace with God? If not, I need to confess and return back to fellowship, then I can present my request to Him.

4. Unity of Spirit with the Brethren

Is my horizontal relationship ok with my fellow brethren? Am I holding unto a grudge? Have I forgiven those who have done me wrong? Do I see myself better than others?

I must begin a reconciliation effort today to clear the air for God to intervene on my behalf.

6. Pride

Pride is defined as feeling or deep pleasure or satisfaction derived from one's own achievements, the achievements of those with whom one is closely associated, or from qualities or possessions that are widely admired. **Pride** means having a feeling of being good and worthy without any credit given to all the other people in your life and the many privileges present in your life. Pride is in fact a sin because it is selfish sense of self-worth. In actuality *pride* means that someone has an unthankful self-made isolated view of their own worth. Pride is a show stopper, any day any time in God. God humbles the proud and gives grace to the humble.

Conclusion and prayer

God sees His house as a house of prayer. It means He is listening and He is answering prayers that line up to His will and advancement of His kingdom. We need to be ready to say YES to this to begin with and everything else falls in line. Sin will no longer have dominion in our lives, we will seek harmony with Him and our other brethren. Everything we do and say will seek to advance His will and His kingdom. Pride will not find a place in us and He will give us the grace to follow through to the very end. In closing, **God's answers are not always aligned with what we think we need but always with a view to what we really do need.**

Dear Lord God, thank You for You told us over and over again that Your house is a house of prayer for all people. Lord, today, in Christ, You have made Your home in us Your people. Help us to walk in the consciousness that we are prayer walking in season and out of season in Jesus name. May answers come speedily as we say YES to Your will and Your kingdom. We pray for the sick or those who are going through certain challenges today, Lord, visit them with Your everlasting arms and we cause a turnaround today in their circumstances and situations to the glory of Your name. Show them, tell them in uncertain ways what is holding back answers so that they can make amends and receive from You that which You already made available to them, In Jesus name we have prayed with thanksgiving, Amen

Shalom!

Monday Ogwuojo Ogbe – E-discipleship

Chapter 22 - The Christian Church – The Powerful Force of Unconditional Love –The Greatest Unending Force the Church Seldom Uses

Introduction

We are exploring the greatest force we have that we seldom use as we reach out (engage) with each other and the world for Christ.. The battle for the souls of men and women within us and around us starts from the banner of love that we exercise within us and around us ..Jesus said in **John 13:34-35**

34 "A new command I give you: Love one another. As I have loved you, so you must love one another. 35 By this everyone will know that you are my disciples, if you love one another."

NUGGETS OF WISDOM

If you only love the lovable, do you expect a pat on the back? *Run-of-the-mill-sinners* do that...check out Luke 6:32-36 in context.

Key verses

1 John 4:8 Amplified Bible (AMP)
8 The one who does not love has not become acquainted with God [does not and never did know Him], for God is

love. [He is the originator of love, and it is an enduring attribute of His nature.]

Deuteronomy 7:6-8 Amplified Bible (AMP)
[6] For you are a holy people [set apart] to the Lord your God; the Lord your God has chosen you out of all the peoples on the face of the earth to be a people for His own possession [that is, His very special treasure]. [7] "The Lord did not love you and choose you because you were greater in number than any of the *other* peoples, for you were the fewest of all peoples. [8] But because the Lord loves you and is keeping the oath which He swore to your fathers, the Lord has brought you out with a mighty hand and redeemed (bought) you from the house of slavery, from the hand of Pharaoh king of Egypt.

Luke 6:32-36 The Message (MSG)
[31-34] "Here is a simple rule of thumb for behavior: Ask yourself what you want people to do for you; then grab the initiative and do it for *them*! If you only love the lovable, do you expect a pat on the back? Run-of-the-mill sinners do that. If you only help those who help you, do you expect a medal? Garden-variety sinners do that. If you only give for what you hope to get out of it, do you think that's charity? The stingiest of pawnbrokers does that.
[35-36] "I tell you, love your enemies. Help and give without expecting a return. You'll never—I promise—regret it. Live out this God-created identity the way our Father lives toward us, generously and graciously, even when we're at our worst. Our Father is kind; you be kind.

John 3:14-17 Amplified Bible (AMP)

14 Just as Moses lifted up the [bronze] serpent in the desert [on a pole], so must the Son of Man be lifted up [on the cross], 15 so that whoever believes will in Him have eternal life [after physical death, and will actually live forever].

16 "For God so [greatly] loved *and* dearly prized the world, that He [even] gave His [One and] [a]only begotten Son, so that whoever believes *and* trusts in Him [as Savior] shall not perish, but have eternal life. 17 For God did not send the Son into the world to judge *and* condemn the world [that is, to initiate the final judgment of the world], but that the world might be saved through Him.

Mark 12:31

This is the second: 'You shall [unselfishly] love your neighbor as yourself.' There is no other commandment greater than these."

John 15:13
No one has greater love [nor stronger commitment] than to lay down his own life for his friends.

1 Corinthians 12:31
But earnestly desire *and* strive for the **greater** gifts [if acquiring them is going to be your goal]. And yet I will show you a still more excellent way [one of the choicest graces and the highest of them all: unselfish **love**].

1 Corinthians 13:1-8 Amplified Bible (AMP)
The Excellence of Love
13 If I speak with the tongues of men and of angels, but have not [a]love [for others growing out of God's love for me], then I have become only a noisy gong or a clanging

cymbal [just an annoying distraction]. [2] And if I have *the gift of* prophecy [and speak a new message from God to the people], and understand all mysteries, and [possess] all knowledge; and if I have all [sufficient] faith so that I can remove mountains, but do not have love [reaching out to others], I am nothing. [3] If I give all my possessions to feed *the poor*, and if I surrender my body [b]to be burned, but do not have love, it does me no good at all.

[4] Love endures with patience *and* serenity, love is kind *and* thoughtful, and is not jealous *or* envious; love does not brag and is not proud *or* arrogant. [5] It is not rude; it is not self-seeking, it is not provoked [nor overly sensitive and easily angered]; it does not take into account a wrong *endured*. [6] It does not rejoice at injustice, but rejoices with the truth [when right and truth prevail]. [7] Love bears all things [regardless of what comes], believes all things [looking for the best in each one], hopes all things [remaining steadfast during difficult times], endures all things [without weakening].

[8] Love never fails [it never fades nor ends]. But as for prophecies, they will pass away; as for tongues, they will cease; as for the gift of special knowledge, it will pass away.

1 Corinthians 1:12,13 New Living Translation

[12] Some of you are saying, "I am a follower of Paul"; and others say that they are for Apollos or for Peter; and some that they alone are the true followers of Christ. [13] **And so, in effect, you have broken Christ into many pieces.** But did I, Paul, die for your sins? Were any of you baptized in my name?

John 13:34-35 Amplified Bible (AMP)
[34] I am giving you a new commandment, that you [a]love one another. Just as I have loved you, so you too are to love one another. [35] By this everyone will know that you are My disciples, if you have love *and* unselfish concern for one another."

Love

Love is made up of three unconditional properties in equal measure:

Acceptance, Understanding and Appreciation
Remove any one of the three and the triangle falls apart. Lets look indebt into the three and how it plays out in the unconditional love Christ has called as ambassadors of His here on earth. Lets begin..

Acceptance

Acceptance is the process or fact of being received as adequate, valid, or suitable. synonyms: welcome, welcoming, favourable reception, embracing, embrace, approval, adoption, integration. We cannot say we have unconditional love if we accept some and reject some. If we do that, we get into the realm of conditions and Gods kind of love get throne off the window.

Paul nailed this home in **Romans 5:8 Amplified Bible (AMP)** [8] **But God clearly shows *and* proves His own love**

for us, by the fact that while we were still sinners, Christ died for us.

Understanding

Understanding means sympathetic awareness or tolerance.
synonyms: compassion, sympathy, pity, empathy, feeling, concern, considerateness, consideration, tenderness, tender-heartedness, kindness, kind-heartedness, sensitivity, insight, fellow feeling, brotherly love, neighbourliness, decency, humanity, humanitarianism, humaneness, charity, goodwill, mercy, mercifulness, gentleness, tolerance, lenience, leniency, warmth, warm-heartedness, affection, love.
God treats us with great kindness and understanding because He knows our form, hence willingness to forgive our wrong doings.
Matthew 16:8-9

But Jesus, aware of this, said, "You men of little faith, why do you discuss among yourselves that you have no bread? "Do you not yet understand or remember the five loaves of the five thousand, and how many baskets full you picked up?

And 1 John 5:20

And we know that the Son of God has come, and has given us understanding so that we may know Him who is true; and we are in Him who is true, in His Son Jesus Christ This is the true God and eternal life.

When we deal with people with the understanding heart by which Christ gives, our engagement changes trajectory for good and for God.

Appreciation

Appreciation means recognition
synonyms: valuing, respect, prizing, cherishing, treasuring, admiration, regard, esteem, high opinion. When we place value on people, the soul God greated for a purpose, our perspective changes dramatically. When we look at the ultimate aim and purpose which transcend the present circumstances, we begin to see the way God sees the people we engage with. Jesus died because of the value He placed on the human soul, so must we.

John 15:13
"Greater love has no one than this, that one lay down his life for his friends
1 Thessalonians 5:12
But we request of you, brethren, that you appreciate those who diligently labor among you, and have charge over you in the Lord and give you instruction,

Conclusion and prayer

Sometimes we ask ourselves if God has sent us into the world, what tools do we have to **initiate, sustain and finish** this work that He has given unto us His ambassadors? Yes we have the Holy Spirit, Yes we have angels, Yes we have disciples plenty too but all of these are useless without the force of LOVE which is God for God is love. Let us engage with this Force of Love this week as we engage the world for Christ.

Dear Lord God, You asked us to love one another as You have loved us. Help us by divine enablement to represent You correctly as we engage with the souls of children, women and men. May they see You in us in all our undertaking in this side of eternity in Jesus name, amen

Shalom!

Chapter 23 - He Christian Church – Questions About Life, Death And The Hereafter – Does God Keep The Church In The Dark? Absolutely Not

Introduction

We are exploring the question about life, especially death and the hereafter. Does God really keep us in the dark about physical and spiritual things? Check the scriptures from Genesis to Revelation and to this present day how God continues to lavish us His children with abundant information to help us appreciate and accept who He is, His plans and desires for mankind and the fact that He is still speaking if we care to listen, pay attention and take necessary steps, we will experience His awesomeness in our day and age. More importantly, we will experience His peace which surpasses all understanding.

NUGGETS OF WISDOM

God is still SPEAKING, WORKING, REVEALING and DOING awesome things in our midst...God always checks my heart not my head for authenticity of my quest for answers to what i don't know or understand...If it is not important to me, He will not volunteer the information. Even when He does by His grace, i will not pick it up...How important is it to me? My thoughts are drawn from Jeremiah 33:2-3 and *Jeremiah 29:12-14* [12] *"When you call on me, when you come and pray to me, I'll listen.* [13-14] *"When you come looking for me, you'll find me.*

"Yes, when you get serious about finding me and want it more than anything else, I'll make sure you won't be disappointed." God's Decree.
"I'll turn things around for you. I'll bring you back from all the countries into which I drove you"—God's Decree—
"bring you home to the place from which I sent you off into exile. You can count on it. – Monday Ogwuojo Ogbe

Key verses

Jeremiah 33:2-5 The Message (MSG)
Things You Could Never Figure Out on Your Own
33 While Jeremiah was still locked up in jail, a second Message from God was given to him:
2-3 "This is God's Message, the God who made earth, made it livable and lasting, known everywhere as *God*: 'Call to me and I will answer you. I'll tell you marvelous and wondrous things that you could never figure out on your own.'
4-5 "This is what God, the God of Israel, has to say about what's going on in this city, about the homes of both people and kings that have been demolished, about all the ravages of war and the killing by the Chaldeans, and about the streets littered with the dead bodies of those killed because of my raging anger—about all that's happened because the evil actions in this city have turned my stomach in disgust.

Mark 12:25-27 The Message (MSG)
24-27 Jesus said, "You're way off base, and here's why: One, you don't know your Bibles; two, you don't know how God works. After the dead are raised up, we're past

the marriage business. As it is with angels now, all our ecstasies and intimacies then will be with God. And regarding the dead, whether or not they are raised, don't you ever read the Bible? How God at the bush said to Moses, 'I am—not *was*—the God of Abraham, the God of Isaac, and the God of Jacob'? The living God is God of the *living*, not the dead. You're way, way off base."

John 14: 1 – 31 The Message (MSG)
The Road

14 ¹⁻⁴ "Don't let this throw you. You trust God, don't you? Trust me. There is plenty of room for you in my Father's home. If that weren't so, would I have told you that I'm on my way to get a room ready for you? And if I'm on my way to get your room ready, I'll come back and get you so you can live where I live. And you already know the road I'm taking."

⁵ Thomas said, "Master, we have no idea where you're going. How do you expect us to know the road?"

⁶⁻⁷ Jesus said, "I am the Road, also the Truth, also the Life. No one gets to the Father apart from me. If you really knew me, you would know my Father as well. From now on, you do know him. You've even seen him!"

⁸ Philip said, "Master, show us the Father; then we'll be content."

⁹⁻¹⁰ "You've been with me all this time, Philip, and you still don't understand? To see me is to see the Father. So how can you ask, 'Where is the Father?' Don't you believe that I am in the Father and the Father is in me? The words that I speak to you aren't mere words. I don't just make them up on my own. The Father who resides in me crafts each word into a divine act.

11-14 "Believe me: I am in my Father and my Father is in me. If you can't believe that, believe what you see—these works. The person who trusts me will not only do what I'm doing but even greater things, because I, on my way to the Father, am giving you the same work to do that I've been doing. You can count on it. From now on, whatever you request along the lines of who I am and what I am doing, I'll do it. That's how the Father will be seen for who he is in the Son. I mean it. Whatever you request in this way, I'll do.

15-17 "If you love me, show it by doing what I've told you. I will talk to the Father, and he'll provide you another Friend so that you will always have someone with you. This Friend is the Spirit of Truth. The godless world can't take him in because it doesn't have eyes to see him, doesn't know what to look for. But you know him already because he has been staying with you, and will even be *in* you!

18-20 "I will not leave you orphaned. I'm coming back. In just a little while the world will no longer see me, but you're going to see me because I am alive and you're about to come alive. At that moment you will know absolutely that I'm in my Father, and you're in me, and I'm in you.

21 "The person who knows my commandments and keeps them, that's who loves me. And the person who loves me will be loved by my Father, and I will love him and make myself plain to him."

22 Judas (not Iscariot) said, "Master, why is it that you are about to make yourself plain to us but not to the world?"

23-24 "Because a loveless world," said Jesus, "is a sightless world. If anyone loves me, he will carefully keep my word and my Father will love him—we'll move right into the neighborhood! Not loving me means not keeping my words. The message you are hearing isn't mine. It's the message of the Father who sent me.

25-27 "I'm telling you these things while I'm still living with you. The Friend, the Holy Spirit whom the Father will send at my request, will make everything plain to you. He will remind you of all the things I have told you. I'm leaving you well and whole. That's my parting gift to you. Peace. I don't leave you the way you're used to being left—feeling abandoned, bereft. So don't be upset. Don't be distraught. 28 "You've heard me tell you, 'I'm going away, and I'm coming back.' If you loved me, you would be glad that I'm on my way to the Father because the Father is the goal and purpose of my life.

29-31 "I've told you this ahead of time, before it happens, so that when it does happen, the confirmation will deepen your belief in me. I'll not be talking with you much more like this because the chief of this godless world is about to attack. But don't worry—he has nothing on me, no claim on me. But so the world might know how thoroughly I love the Father, I am carrying out my Father's instructions right down to the last detail.

"Get up. Let's go. It's time to leave here."

1 Corinthians 15:51-57 The Message (MSG)
51-57 But let me tell you something wonderful, a mystery I'll probably never fully understand. We're not all going to die—*but* we are all going to be changed. You hear a blast to end all blasts from a trumpet, and in the time that you look up and blink your eyes—it's over. On signal from that trumpet from heaven, the dead will be up and out of their graves, beyond the reach of death, never to die again. At the same moment and in the same way, we'll all be changed. In the resurrection scheme of things, this has to happen: everything perishable taken off the shelves and

replaced by the imperishable, this mortal replaced by the immortal. Then the saying will come true:
Death swallowed by triumphant Life!
Who got the last word, oh, Death?
Oh, Death, who's afraid of you now?
It was sin that made death so frightening and law-code guilt that gave sin its leverage, its destructive power. But now in a single victorious stroke of Life, all three—sin, guilt, death—are gone, the gift of our Master, Jesus Christ. Thank God!

1 Corinthians 1:12,13 New Living Translation

[12] Some of you are saying, "I am a follower of Paul"; and others say that they are for Apollos or for Peter; and some that they alone are the true followers of Christ. [13] **And so, in effect, you have broken Christ into many pieces.**
But did I, Paul, die for your sins? Were any of you baptized in my name?

John 13:34-35 Amplified Bible (AMP)

[34] I am giving you a new commandment, that you [a]love one another. Just as I have loved you, so you too are to love one another. [35] By this everyone will know that you are My disciples, if you have love *and* unselfish concern for one another."

John 17:20-26 The Message (MSG)
Jesus' Prayer for His Followers

[20-23] I'm praying not only for them
But also for those who will believe in me
Because of them and their witness about me.
The goal is for all of them to become one heart and mind—

Just as you, Father, are in me and I in you,
So they might be one heart and mind with us.
Then the world might believe that you, in fact, sent me.
The same glory you gave me, I gave them,
So they'll be as unified and together as we are—
I in them and you in me.
Then they'll be mature in this oneness,
And give the godless world evidence
That you've sent me and loved them
In the same way you've loved me.
24-26 Father, I want those you gave me
To be with me, right where I am,
So they can see my glory, the splendor you gave me,
Having loved me
Long before there ever was a world.
Righteous Father, the world has never known you,
But I have known you, and these disciples know
That you sent me on this mission.
I have made your very being known to them—
Who you are and what you do—
And continue to make it known,
So that your love for me
Might be in them
Exactly as I am in them.

Matthew 17:1-8 The Message (MSG)
Sunlight Poured from His Face

17 1-3 Six days later, three of them saw that glory. Jesus took Peter and the brothers, James and John, and led them up a high mountain. His appearance changed from the inside out, right before their eyes. Sunlight poured from his face. His clothes were filled with light. Then they realized that Moses and Elijah were also there in deep conversation with him.

[4] Peter broke in, "Master, this is a great moment! What would you think if I built three memorials here on the mountain—one for you, one for Moses, one for Elijah?" [5] While he was going on like this, babbling, a light-radiant cloud enveloped them, and sounding from deep in the cloud a voice: "This is my Son, marked by my love, focus of my delight. Listen to him." [6-8] When the disciples heard it, they fell flat on their faces, scared to death. But Jesus came over and touched them. "Don't be afraid." When they opened their eyes and looked around all they saw was Jesus, only Jesus

Revelation 22:1-13 The Message (MSG)

22 [1-5] Then the Angel showed me Water-of-Life River, crystal bright. It flowed from the Throne of God and the Lamb, right down the middle of the street. The Tree of Life was planted on each side of the River, producing twelve kinds of fruit, a ripe fruit each month. The leaves of the Tree are for healing the nations. Never again will anything be cursed. The Throne of God and of the Lamb is at the center. His servants will offer God service—worshiping, they'll look on his face, their foreheads mirroring God. Never again will there be any night. No one will need lamplight or sunlight. The shining of God, the Master, is all the light anyone needs. And they will rule with him age after age after age.
[6-7] The Angel said to me, "These are dependable and accurate words, every one. The God and Master of the spirits of the prophets sent his Angel to show his servants what must take place, and soon. And tell them, 'Yes, I'm on my way!' Blessed be the one who keeps the words of the prophecy of this book."
[8-9] I, John, saw all these things with my own eyes, heard them with my ears. Immediately when I heard and saw, I

fell on my face to worship at the feet of the Angel who laid it all out before me. He objected, "No you don't! I'm a servant just like you and your companions, the prophets, and all who keep the words of this book. Worship God!" 10-11 The Angel continued, "Don't seal the words of the prophecy of this book; don't put it away on the shelf. Time is just about up. Let evildoers do their worst and the dirty-minded go all out in pollution, but let the righteous maintain a straight course and the holy continue on in holiness."

12-13 "Yes, I'm on my way! I'll be there soon! I'm bringing my payroll with me. I'll pay all people in full for their life's work. I'm A to Z, the First and the Final, Beginning and Conclusion.

Deuteronomy 29:29 English Standard Version (ESV)
29 "The secret things belong to the Lord our God, but the things that are revealed belong to us and to our children forever, that we may do all the words of this law.

News about events from around the world

We are inundated with news of wars and rumors of wars, earthquakes, kidnap, terrorism, rigging of elections, corruption, BREXIT, impeachments, trade wars, church splits, building collapse and the latest crash of the Ethiopian airline with 157 souls and we seems not to be able to make sense of it all. In all of the confusion, it is easy to loss site of God and His eternal plans. I want to draw our attention to what He is saying today and through eternity...read these from the Fathers heart through various messengers as we navigate the ever changing and tempestuous world around us.

- 1) "Pride is the hardest enemy to see, and it always sneaks up behind you," "In some ways, those who have been to the greatest heights are in the greatest danger of falling. You must always remember that in this life you can fall at any time from any level. 'Take heed when you think you stand, lest you fall,' When you think you are the least vulnerable to falling is in fact when you are the most vulnerable. Most men fall right after a great victory."

- 2) "Stay close to me, inquire of the Lord before making any major decisions, and keep that mantle on, and the enemy will never be able to blindside you as he did those."

- 3) "The Lord is closer to the homeless than to princes. You only have true strength to the degree that you walk in the grace of God, and 'He gives His grace to the humble.' No enemy weapon can penetrate this mantle, because nothing can overpower His grace. As long as you wear this mantle you are safe from this kind of attack."

- 4) "I told you that I would never leave you or forsake you. I am with all of My warriors just as I am with you. I will be to you whatever you need to accomplish My will, and you have needed wisdom."

- 5) True worship also pours the precious oil upon the Head, Jesus, which then flows down over the entire body, making us one with Him and each other. No one who becomes one with Him will remain wounded or unclean. His blood is pure life, and it flows when we are joined to Him. When we are joined to Him we are also joined to the rest of the body, so that His blood flows through all. Is that not how you heal a wound to your body, by closing the wound so that the blood can flow to the wounded member to bring regeneration? When a part of His body is wounded, we must join in unity with that part until it is fully restored. We are all one in Him."

- 6) "We are not complete, and our worship is not complete, until the whole body is restored. Even in the most glorious worship, even in the very presence of the King, we will all feel this emptiness until all are one, because our King also feels it. We all grieve for our brothers in bondage, but we grieve even more for the heart of our King. Just as you love all of your children, but would be grieved for the one that was sick or wounded, He too loves all of His children, but the wounded and oppressed have most of His attention now. For His sake we must not quit until all have been recovered. As long as any are wounded, He is wounded."

-

- 7) "You are wise to doubt yourself. But true faith depends on God, not yourself, and not your faith. You are close to the kind of faith that can move this mountain, and move it must. It is time to carry it to places that it has not gone to before.

- 8) "The Lord gave us a map to His kingdom when He said, 'If you seek to save your life you will lose it, but if you will lose your life for My sake you will find it.'

- 9) "God has a different definition of peace and safety than we do. To be wounded in the fight is a great honor. That is why the apostle Paul boasted of his beatings and stonings. There is no courage unless there is real danger. The Lord said He would go with Joshua to fight for the Promised Land, but over and over exhorted him to be strong and courageous because he was going to have to fight, and there would be dangers. It is in this way the Lord proves those

who are worthy of the Promises-they love God and His provision more than their own security. Courage is a demonstration of true faith. The Lord never promised that His way would be easy, but it would be worth it. The courage of those who fought from the level of Salvation moved the angels of heaven to esteem what God has wrought in the fallen race of men. They took their wounds in the terrible onslaught, but they did not quit, and they did not retreat. Even so, by climbing the mountain you were able to fight with an authority that ultimately freed even more souls. Many more souls will fill these rooms, to the great joy of heaven, if you go on."

Account Of Those Who Have Gone Ahead Of Us

10) "Everyone here knows you, and all of those who are now fighting on the earth. We are the saints who have served the Lord in the generations before you. We are the great cloud of witnesses who have been given the right to behold the last battle. We know all of you, and we see all that you do."

- I then noticed someone I had known on earth. He had been a faithful believer, but I did not think he had done anything of significance. He was so physically unattractive on earth that it had made him shy. Here he had the same features, but was somehow more handsome than any person I had known on earth. He stepped up to me with an assurance and dignity that I had never seen in him, or anyone, before.
- "Heaven is much greater than we could have dreamed while on earth," he began. "This room is but the threshold of realms of glory that are far beyond the ability we had to comprehend. It is also true that the second death is much more terrible than we understood. Neither heaven or hell are like we thought they were. If I had known on earth what I know here I would not have lived the way that I did. You are blessed with a great grace to have come here before you have died." he said while looking at my garments.

- 11) "We have our incorruptible bodies now, and you do not. Our minds are no longer hindered by sin. We are therefore able to comprehend many times what even the greatest earthly mind can fathom, and we will spend eternity growing in our ability to understand. This is so that we can know the Father, and understand the glory of His creation. On earth you cannot even begin to understand what the least of these here know, and we are the least of those here."
- "How could you be the least?" I asked with disbelief.
- "There is an aristocracy here. The rewards for our earthly lives are the eternal positions that we have here. This great multitude here are those whom the Lord called 'foolish virgins.' We knew the Lord, and trusted in His cross for deliverance from damnation, but we did not really live for Him, but for ourselves. We did not keep our vessels filled with the oil of the Holy Spirit. We have eternal life, but we wasted our lives on earth."
- I was really surprised by this, but I also knew that no one could lie in that place. "The foolish virgins gnashed their teeth in the outer darkness," I protested.
- "And that we did. The grief that we experienced when we understood how we had so wasted our lives was beyond any grief possible on earth. The darkness of that grief can only be understood by those who have experienced it. Such darkness is magnified when it is revealed next to the glory of the One we failed. You are standing now among the lowest rank in heaven. There are no greater

fools than the ones who know the great salvation of God, but then go on living for themselves. To come here and learn the reality of that folly is a grief beyond what an earthly soul can experience. We are those who suffered this outer darkness because of this greatest of follies."

- I was still incredulous. "But you are more glorious and full of more joy and peace than I even imagined, even for those in heaven. I do not feel any remorse in you, and yet I know that here you cannot lie. This does not make sense to me."

- Looking me straight in the eyes, he continued, "The Lord also loves us with a love greater than you can yet understand. Before His judgment seat I tasted the greatest darkness of soul and remorse that can be experienced. Though here we do not measure time as you do, it seemed to last for as long as my life on earth had lasted. All of my sins and follies which I had not repented of passed before me, and before all who are here. The grief of this you cannot understand until you have experienced it. I felt that I was in the deepest dungeon of hell, even as I stood before the Lord. He was resolute until my life had been completely reviewed. When I said I was sorry and asked for the mercy of His cross, He wiped away my tears and took away the great darkness. He looked at me with a love that was beyond anything that you can now understand. He gave me this robe. I no longer feel the darkness or bitterness that I knew as I stood before Him, but I remember it. Only here can you remember such things without continuing to feel the pain. A moment in the lowest part of heaven is much greater than a thousand years of the highest life on earth. Now my mourning at my folly has been turned into joy, and I know that I will know joy forever, even if I am in the lowest place in heaven."

- I began to think again of the treasures of salvation. Somehow I knew that all that this man had told me was revealed by those treasures. Every step I had taken up the mountain, or into it, had revealed that His ways are both more fearful and more wonderful than I had known before.

- Looking at me intently, my former acquaintance continued. "You are not here to understand, but to experience. The next level of rank here is many times greater than what we have. Each level after is that much greater than the previous one. It is not just that each level has an even more glorious spiritual body, but that each level is closer to the throne where all of the glory comes from. Even so, I no longer feel the grief of my failure. I really deserve nothing. I am here by grace alone, and I am so thankful for what I have. He is so worthy to be loved. I could be doing many wondrous things now in the different realms of heaven, but I would rather stay here and just behold the glory, even if I am on the outer fringes."

- Then, with a distant look in his eyes, he added, "Everyone in heaven is now in this room to watch His great mystery unfold, and to watch those of you who will fight the last battle." "Can you see Him from here?" I asked. "I see His glory far away, but I cannot see Him."

- "I can see many times better than you can," he answered. "And yes, I can see Him, and all that He is doing, even from here. I can also hear Him. I can also behold the earth. He gave us all that power. We are the great cloud of witnesses who are beholding you."

- He departed back into the ranks and I began walking again, trying to understand all that he had said to me. As I looked over the great host that he had said were the foolish virgins, the ones who had spiritually slept away their life on earth, I knew that if any one of them appeared on earth now that they would be worshiped as gods, and yet they were the very least of those who were here!

- I then began to think of all of the time that I had wasted in my life. It was such an overwhelming thought that I stopped. Then parts of my life began to pass before me. I began to experience a terrible grief over this one sin. I too had been one of the greatest of fools! I may have kept more oil in my lamp than others, but now I knew how foolish I had been to measure what was required of me by how others were doing. I, too, was one of the foolish virgins!

- 12) Just when I thought I would collapse under the weight of this terrible discovery, a man who I had known and esteemed as one of the great men of God I had known, came forward to steady me. Somehow his touch revived me. He then greeted me warmly. He was a man that I had wanted to be discipled by. I had met him, but we did not get along well. Like a number of others I had tried to get close enough to learn from, I was an irritation to him and he finally asked me to leave. For years I had felt guilty about this, feeling that I had missed a great opportunity because of some flaw in my character. Even though I had put it out of my mind, I still carried the weight of this failure. When I saw him it all surfaced, and a sick feeling came over me. Now he was so regal that I felt even more repulsive and embarrassed by my poor state. I wanted to hide but there was no way I could avoid him here. To my surprise, his warmth toward me was so genuine that he quickly put me at ease. There did not seem to be any barriers between us. In fact, the love I felt coming from him almost completely took away my self-consciousness.

- "I have waited eagerly for this meeting," he said. "You were waiting for me?" I asked. "Why?"

- "You are just one of many that I am waiting for. I did not understand until my judgment that you were one that I was called to help, to even disciple, but I rejected you."

- "Sir," I protested. "It would have been a great honor to be discipled by you, and I am very thankful for the time that I did have with you, but I was so arrogant I deserved your rejection. I know that my rebellion and pride has kept me from ever having a real spiritual father. This was not your fault, but mine."

- "It is true that you were prideful, but that is not why I was offended with you. I was offended because of my insecurity, which made me want to control everyone around me. I was offended that you would not accept everything that I said without questioning it. I then started to look for anything that was wrong with you to justify my rejection. I began to feel that if I could not control

263

you that you would one day embarrass me and my ministry. I esteemed my ministry more than I did the people for whom it was given to me, so I drove many like you away," he said.

- With a genuineness that is unknown in the realms of earth, he continued, "All children are rebellious, and think that the world revolves around them. That is why they need parents to raise them. Almost every child will at times bring reproach on his family, but he is still a part of the family. I turned away many of God's own children that he had entrusted to me for getting them safely to maturity. I failed with most of them. Most of them suffered terrible wounds and failures that I could have helped them to avoid. Many of them are now prisoners of the enemy. I built a large organization, and had considerable influence in the church, but the greatest gifts that the Lord trusted to me were the ones who were sent to me for discipline, many of whom I rejected. Had I not been so self-centered and concerned with my own reputation I would be a king here. I was called to one of the highest thrones. All that you have and will accomplish would have been in my heavenly account as well. Instead, much of what I gave my attention to was of very little true eternal significance. What looks good on earth looks very different here. What will make you a king on earth will often be a stumbling block to keep you from being a king here. What will make you a king here is lowly and un- esteemed on earth. Will you forgive me?"

- "Of course," I said, quite embarrassed. "But I, too, am in need of your forgiveness. I still think that it was my awkwardness and rebellion that made it difficult for you."

- "It is true that you were not perfect, and I discerned some of your problems rightly, but that is never cause for rejection," he replied. "The Lord did not reject the world when I saw its failures. He did not reject me when He saw my sin. He laid down His life for us. It is always the greater who must lay down his life for the lesser. I was more mature. I had more authority than you, but I became like one of the goats in the parable; I rejected the Lord by rejecting you and the others that He sent to me."

- As he talked, his words were striking me deeply. I, too, was guilty of everything that he was relenting of. Many young men and women who I had brushed off as not being important enough for my time were now passing through my mind. How desperately I wanted to return now and gather them together! This grief that I began to feel was even worse than I had felt about wasting time. I had wasted people! Now many of these were prisoners of the enemy, wounded and captured during the battle on the mountain. This whole battle was for people, and yet people were often regarded as the least important. We will fight for truths more than for the people for whom they are given. We will fight for ministries while running roughshod over the people in them. "And many people think of me as a spiritual leader! I am truly the least of the saints," I thought to myself.

- "I understand how you feel," remarked another man I recognized as one I considered one of the greatest Christian leaders of all time. "Paul the apostle said near the end of his life that he was the least of the saints. Then just before his death he even called himself 'the greatest of sinners.' Had he not learned that in his life on earth he, too, would have been in jeopardy of being one of the least of the saints in heaven. Because he learned it on earth he is now one of those closest to the Lord, and will be one of the highest in rank for all of eternity."

- Seeing this man in the company of "The foolish virgins" was the greatest surprise I had yet. "I cannot believe that you, too, are one of the foolish who slept away their lives on earth. Why are you here?"

- "I am here because I made one of the most grave mistakes you can make as one entrusted with the glorious gospel of our Savior. Just as the apostle Paul progressed from not considering himself inferior to the greatest apostles, to being the greatest of sinners, I took the opposite course. I started out knowing that I had been one the greatest of sinners who had found grace, but ended up thinking that I was one of the greatest apostles. It was because of my great pride, not insecurity like our friend here, that I began to attack everyone who did not see everything just the way I did. Those who followed me I stripped of their own callings, and even their personalities, pressuring them to all become just like me. No one around me could be themselves. No one dared to question me because I would crush them into powder; I thought that by making others smaller I made myself larger. I thought that I was supposed to be the Holy Spirit to everyone. From the outside my ministry looked like a smooth running machine where everyone was in unity and there was perfect order, but it was the order of a concentration camp. I took the Lord's own children and made them automatons in my own image instead of His. In the end I was not even serving the Lord, but the idol I had built to myself. By the end of my life I was actually an enemy of the true gospel, at least in practice, even if my teachings and writings seemed impeccably biblical."

- "If that is true, that you became an enemy of the gospel, how is it that you are still here?" I questioned.

- "By the grace of God, I did trust in the cross for my own salvation, even though I actually kept other men from it, leading them to myself rather than to Him. The Lord remains faithful to us even when we are unfaithful. It was also by His grace that the Lord took me from the earth sooner than He would have just so those who were under me could find Him and come to know Him."

- I could not have been more stunned to think that this was true of this particular man. History had given us a very different picture of him. Reading what was going on in my heart, he continued:

- "God does have a different set of history books than those on the earth. You have had a glimpse of this, but you do not yet know how different they are. Earthly histories will pass away, but the books that are kept here will last forever. If you can rejoice in what heaven is recording about your life, you are blessed indeed. Men see through a glass darkly, so their histories will always be clouded, and sometimes completely wrong. Very few, even very few Christians, have the true gift of discernment. Without this gift it is impossible to accurately discern truth in those of the present or the past. Even with this gift it is difficult. Until you have been here, and been stripped, you will judge others through distorted prejudices, either positive or negative. That is why we were warned not to judge before the time. Until we have been here we just cannot really know what is in the heart of others, whether they are performing good or evil deeds. There have been good motives in even the worst of men, and evil motives in even the best of them. Only here can men be judged by both their deeds and their motives."

- "When I return to earth, will I be able to discern history accurately because I have been here?"
- "You are here because you prayed for the Lord to judge you severely, to correct you ruthlessly, so that you could serve Him more perfectly. This was one of the most wise requests you ever made. The wise judge themselves lest they be judged. The even wiser ask for the judgments of the Lord, because they realize that they cannot even judge themselves very well. Having come here you will leave with far more wisdom and discernment, but on earth you will always see through a glass darkly to at least some degree. Your experience here will help you to know men better, but only when you are fully here can you know them fully. When you leave here you will be more impressed by how little you know men rather than by how well you know them. This is just as true in relation

to the histories of men. I have been allowed to talk with you because I have in a sense discipled you through my writings, and to know the truth about me will help you greatly," the great Reformer concluded.

Conclusion and prayer

Drawing from our nuggets of wisdom today we conclude with this as you review the twelve key messages above and take corrective action in this part of eternity ... God is still SPEAKING, WORKING, REVEALING and DOING awesome things in our midst...God always checks my heart not my head for authenticity of my quest for answers to what i don't know or understand...If it is not important to me, He will not volunteer the information. Even when He does by His grace, i will not pick it up...How important is it to me? My thoughts are drawn from Jeremiah 33:2-3 and *Jeremiah 29:12-14* [12] *"When you call on me, when you come and pray to me, I'll listen.* [13-14] *"When you come looking for me, you'll find me.* *"Yes, when you get serious about finding me and want it more than anything else, I'll make sure you won't be disappointed." God's Decree.*
"I'll turn things around for you. I'll bring you back from all the countries into which I drove you"—God's Decree—

"bring you home to the place from which I sent you off into exile. You can count on it.

Dear Lord God, reveal Yourself and Your mysteries to those who REALLY seek You in truth for answers to questions that have troubled them through life. Help us all to draw inspiration from the twelve (12) messages above through the ages by the hands of messengers in our midst in Jesus name, amen

Shalom!

Monday Ogwuojo Ogbe – E-discipleship

Chapter 24 – Conclusion

In concluding, I will bring some highlight to the book borderless.
We have said and written a lot on the need for unity in the body of Christ.

We pray that you have gotten the burden by now and are already thinking on how not to be part of the problem but the solution by engaging right away. Engagement states by praying, praying births desire that God Himself will put in our hearts to do His bidding. Commit your ways to the Lord and He will GIVE YOU the desires of your heart...really His own heart desire becomes yours

Proverbs 16:3 Commit thy works unto the LORD, and thy thoughts shall be established.
1. Literally, roll them upon Him, as a burden too heavy to be borne by thyself. " ...
2. Psalm 37:5 **Commit thy way** unto the LORD; trust also in him; and he shall bring it to pass.

Borderless - Envisioning and Experiencing One Church Community of Believers Without Walls, Borders and Denominations

The call to unity is urgent, it is needed not just for ourselves but for those souls that are seeing the division amongst us and would not give their lives to Christ. You will be burdened after reading this book to do something in the mighty name of Jesus Christ, Amen

Borderless is about unity in the body of Christ. It is calling the church to a place of unity of Spirit in response to Jesus prayer that they may be one...John 17:22. A call to our various gathering to strive for unity. That we will all envision a borderless church without walls, borders and denomination. A church that despite diversity will be united in spirit and engage as one as written in Ephesians 4:5-6 King James Version (KJV)

5 One Lord, one faith, one baptism,6 One God and Father of all, who is above all, and through all, and in you all.

No more denominational walls and borders. Just one denomination - Jesus Christ, Our Lord and savior taking His place as the only supreme head of His church. It is an appeal and prayer to unity, to oneness, to love and to one body in one Christ Jesus. I believe by reading Borderless, you have become burdened to the point of engagement with our other brothers and sisters in love in other gathering beyond your own familiar domain, creed, doctrine and denomination. My job will have been dispensed.

RECALL

"Being prideful means having or showing an arrogant superiority to and disdain of that one view as unworthy. Pride can only be found where there is no love. Where there is no love, there is no God because God is love. Our love for God is the root while our love for the brethren is the fruit. Jesus says, a Christian will be known by the fruit of love they manifest. The world will know us by the love we have for one another." – Monday Ogwuojo Ogbe

"A House divided against itself cannot stand - True! Whether it is the family, Church or Nation! May the good Lord show us mercy and cause us to guard against the little foxes that subtly disrupts what is good. We pray for unity of purpose in Jesus name!" – Sola Ogunnaike.

"Thank you, Monday, for this exposition. The church of Jesus Christ need to realize that the greatest message of love we send to the unbelieving world is our working in unity" – Grace Akuh.

"We all need one another to be the complete reflection of Him." – Rick Joyner

"Thank you for taking on the presentation of the church history and how we got divided. I like the rich passages and perceptive insights. They are very useful." – Dr. Daniel Obaka

"Has it ever occurred to you that one hundred pianos all tuned to the same fork are automatically tuned to each other? They are of one accord by being tuned, not to each other, but to another standard to which each one must individually bow. So one hundred worshippers together, each one looking away to Christ, are in heart nearer to each other than they could possibly be were they to become 'unity' conscious and turn their eyes away from God to strive for closer fellowship."- A.W. Tozer, (*The Pursuit of God*)

"It is high time we do something about disunity in the body of Christ. Thank you for sharing information on other Christian groups and how we can connect with them" – Vera Atodo

"A true non-denominational view holds that the body of Christ cannot be and should not be denominated"

"The Father, the Son and the Holy Spirit are one. The Father is not The Son, The Son is not the Holy Spirit, yet they operate and function as one. The Body is not the Spirit, or is the Spirit the mind but in this part of eternity, all three must work together so we can be a complete human being. The man is not the woman, neither is the woman the man but God said, they are one. God is interested in who we are and also interested in what we do with who we are." – Monday Ogwuojo Ogbe

Shalom!

GREAT OPPORTUNITY

We will not end this title on Borderless until we present opportunity to those who have not encountered Jesus to make their peace today

Prayer Of Salvation
Prayer of Salvation - Our First Real Conversation With God

The "prayer of salvation" is the most important prayer we'll ever pray. When we're ready to become a Christian, we're ready to have our first real conversation with God, and these are its components:

- We acknowledge that Jesus Christ is God; that He came to earth as a man in order to live the sinless life that we cannot live; that He died in our place,

so that we would not have to pay the penalty we deserve.
- We confess our past life of sin -- living for ourselves and not obeying God.
- We admit we are ready to trust Jesus Christ as our Savior and Lord.
- We ask Jesus to come into our heart, take up residence there, and begin living through us.

Prayer of Salvation - It Begins With Faith in God

When we pray the prayer of salvation, we're letting God know we believe His Word is true. By the faith He has given us, we choose to believe in Him. The Bible tells us that "*without faith it is impossible to please Him, for he who comes to God must believe that He is, and that He is a rewarder of those who diligently seek Him*" (Hebrews 11:6).

So, when we pray, asking God for the gift of salvation, we're exercising our free will to acknowledge that we believe in Him. That demonstration of faith pleases God, because we have freely chosen to know Him.

Prayer of Salvation - Confessing Our Sin

When we pray the prayer of salvation, we're admitting that we've sinned. As the Bible says of everyone, save Christ alone: "*For all have sinned, and fall short of the glory of God*" (Romans 3:23).

To sin is simply to fall short of the mark, as an arrow that does not quite hit the bull's-eye. The glory of God that we fall short of is found only in Jesus Christ: "*For it is the God* who commanded light to shine out of darkness, who has shone in our hearts to give the light of the knowledge of the glory of God in the face of Jesus Christ" (2 Corinthians 4:6).

The prayer of salvation, then, recognizes that Jesus Christ is the only human who ever lived without sin. "*For He made Him who knew no sin to be sin for us, that we might become the righteousness of God in Him*" (2 Corinthians 5:21).

Prayer of Salvation - Professing Faith in Christ as Savior and Lord

With Christ as our standard of perfection, we're now acknowledging faith in Him as God, agreeing with the Apostle John that: "*In the beginning was the Word (Christ), and the Word was with God, and the Word was God. He was in the beginning with God. All things were made through Him, and without Him nothing was made that was made*" (John 1:1-3).

Because God could only accept a perfect, sinless sacrifice, and because He knew that we could not possibly accomplish that, He sent His Son to die for us and pay the eternal price. "*For God so loved the world that He gave His only begotten Son, that whoever believes in Him should not perish but have everlasting life.*" (John 3:16).

Prayer of Salvation - Say It & Mean It Now!

Do you agree with everything you have read so far? If you do, don't wait a moment longer to start your new life in Jesus Christ. Remember, this prayer is not a magical formula. You are simply expressing your heart to God. Pray this with us:

"Father, I know that I have broken your laws and my sins have separated me from you. I am truly sorry, and now I want to turn away from my past sinful life toward you. Please forgive me, and help me avoid sinning again. I believe that your son, Jesus Christ died for my sins, was resurrected from the dead, is alive, and hears my prayer. I invite Jesus to become the Lord of my life, to rule and reign in my heart from this day forward. Please send your Holy Spirit to help me obey You, and to do Your will for the rest of my life. In Jesus' name I pray, Amen."

Prayer of Salvation - I've Prayed It; Now What?

If you've prayed this prayer of salvation with true conviction and heart, you are now a follower of Jesus. This is a fact, whether or not you feel any different. Religious systems may have led you to believe that you should feel something - a warm glow, a tingle, or some other mystical experience. The fact is, you may, or you may not. If you have prayed the prayer of salvation and meant it, you are now a follower of Jesus. The Bible tells us that your eternal salvation is secure! *"that if you confess with your mouth the Lord Jesus and believe in your heart that God has raised Him from the dead, you will be saved"* (Romans 10:9).

Welcome to the family of God! We encourage you now to find a local church where you can be baptized and grow in the knowledge of God through His Word, the Bible.
You can also visit our site at www.otakada.org that will help you develop and grow in Christ
Using this link in the discovery bible study to discover Jesus for yourself https://www.otakada.org/dbs-dmm/

Or you can begin a 40 days journey at your pace online via this link https://www.otakada.org/get-free-40-days-online-discipleship-course-in-a-journey-with-jesus/

If you need guidance, send an email to info@otakada.org May the Lord expand your life and fill you with joy, peace, love and harmony which only Him can give, amen

Printed in June 2023
by Rotomail Italia S.p.A., Vignate (MI) - Italy